THE COLLECTOR OF
TREASURES

BESSIE HEAD, one of Africa's best-known women writers, was born in South Africa in 1937, the result of an 'illicit' union between a black man and a white woman. Her life was a traumatic one, and she drew heavily upon her own personal experiences for her novels. She was sent to a foster family until she was 13, and then a mission school before training as a teacher. After a few years teaching she left to work as a journalist for *Golden City Post*, a DRUM publication, but an unsuccessful marriage and her involvement in the trial of a friend led her to apply for another teaching post, in Botswana, where she took up permanent exile. She remained there, with the precarious status of 'refugee' for 15 years before she gained citizenship in 1979, and it was in Botswana that Bessie Head died tragically early, aged 49, in 1986.

Botswana is the backdrop for all three of her outstanding novels. *When Rain Clouds Gather*, her first novel, based on her time as a refugee living at the Bamangwato Development Farm, was published in 1969. This was followed by *Maru* (1971) and her intense and powerful autobiographical work *A Question of Power* (1973). *The Collector of Treasures* (1977) was her first collection of short stories, followed in 1981 by *Serowe: Village of the Rain Wind*, a skilful and original historical portrait of 100 years of the Botswanan community, reconstructed through the words of different members of the village, and *A Bewitched Crossroad*, which appeared in 1984. *A Woman Alone* (1990), a collection of Bessie Head's autobiographical writings, and *Tales of Tenderness and Power* (1990), a moving selection of famous and previously unpublished works, have been published posthumously. All her works (except for *A Bewitched Crossroad*) are available in the Heinemann African Writers Series.

BESSIE HEAD

THE COLLECTOR OF TREASURES

and other Botswana Village Tales

HEINEMANN

Heinemann International Literature and Textbooks
A division of Heinemann Educational Books Ltd
Halley Court, Jordan Hill, Oxford OX2 8EJ

Heinemann Educational Books Inc
361 Hanover Street, Portsmouth, New Hampshire, 03801, USA

Heinemann Educational Books (Nigeria) Ltd
PMB 5205, Ibadan
Heinemann Educational Boleswa
PO Box 10103, Village Post Office, Gaborone, Botswana

LONDON   EDINBURGH   PARIS   MADRID
ATHENS   BOLOGNA   MELBOURNE
SYDNEY   AUCKLAND   SINGAPORE   TOKYO

First published by Heinemann Educational Books Ltd
in the African Writers Series in 1977
Reprinted twelve times
First published in this edition by
Heinemann International Literature and Textbooks
in 1992

British Library Cataloguing in Publication Data
A catalogue record for this book is available from the British Library
ISBN 0 435 90981 9

Printed in Great Britain by
Cox & Wyman Ltd, Reading, Berkshire

92 93 94 95   10 9   8   7   6   5   4   3   2   1

For my devoted fans,
Betty Sleath and Gothe Kgamane

CONTENTS

ACKNOWLEDGEMENTS

I acknowledge an indebtedness to Professor C. L. S.
Nyembezi's beautiful interpretations of *Zulu Proverbs*
(Witwatersrand University Press, Johannesburg, 1954), to
which I referred while working on this collection of stories.

Some of the stories previously appeared in *Encounter*,
Essence, The Magazine for Black Women, Black World, and *Ms*
Magazine. 'Witchcraft' appeared in an anthology, *Quarry '76:
New South African Writing* (Ad Donker, Publisher,
Johannesburg 1976).

The Deep River: A Story of Ancient Tribal Migration

Long ago, when the land was only cattle tracks and footpaths, the people lived together like a deep river. In this deep river which was unruffled by conflict or a movement forward, the people lived without faces, except for their chief, whose face was the face of all the people; that is, if their chief's name was Monemapee, then they were all the people of Monemapee. The Talaote tribe have forgotten their origins and their original language during their journey southwards—they have merged and remerged again with many other tribes—and the name, Talaote, is all they have retained in memory of their history. Before a conflict ruffled their deep river, they were all the people of Monemapee, whose kingdom was somewhere in the central part of Africa.

They remembered that Monemapee ruled the tribe for many years as the hairs on his head were already saying white! by the time he died. On either side of the deep river there might be hostile tribes or great dangers, so all the people lived in one great town. The lands where they ploughed their crops were always near the town. That was done by all the tribes for their own protection, and their day-to-day lives granted them no individual faces either for they ploughed their crops, reared their children, and held their festivities according to the laws of the land.

Although the people were given their own ploughing lands, they had no authority to plough them without the chief's order. When the people left home to go to plough, the chief sent out the proclamation for the beginning of the ploughing season. When harvest time came, the chief perceived that the corn was ripe. He gathered the people together and said:

'Reap now, and come home.'

When the people brought home their crops, the chief called the thanksgiving for the harvest. Then the women of the whole town carried their corn in flat baskets, to the chief's place. Some of that corn was accepted on its arrival, but the rest was returned so that the women might soak it in their own yards. After a few days, the chief sent his special messenger to proclaim that the harvest thanksgiving corn was to be pounded. The special messenger went around the whole town and in each place where there was a little hill or mound, he climbed it and shouted:

'Listen, the corn is to be pounded!'

So the people took their sprouting corn and pounded it. After some days the special messenger came back and called out:

'The corn is to be fermented now!'

A few days passed and then he called out:

'The corn is to be cooked now!'

So throughout the whole town the beer was boiled and when it had been strained, the special messenger called out for the last time:

'The beer is to be brought now!'

On the day on which thanksgiving was to be held, the women all followed one another in single file to the chief's place. Large vessels had been prepared at the chief's place, so that when the women came they poured the beer into them. Then there was a gathering of all the people to celebrate thanksgiving for the harvest time. All the people lived this way, like one face, under their chief. They accepted this regimental levelling down of their individual souls, but on the day of dispute or when strife and conflict and greed blew stormy winds over their deep river, the people awoke and showed their individual faces.

Now, during his lifetime Monemapee had had three wives. Of these marriages he had four sons: Sebembele by the senior wife; Ntema and Mosemme by the second junior wife; and Kgagodi by the third junior wife. There was a fifth son, Makobi, a small baby who was still suckling at his mother's breast by the time the old chief, Monemapee, died. This mother was the third junior wife, Rankwana. It was about the fifth son, Makobi, that the dispute arose. There was a secret there. Monemapee had married the third junior wife, Rankwana, late in his years. She was young and beautiful and Sebembele, the senior son, fell in love with her—but in secret. On the death of Monemapee, Sebembele, as senior son, was installed chief of the tribe and immediately made a blunder. He claimed Rankwana as his wife and exposed the secret that the fifth son, Makobi, was his own child and not that of his father.

This news was received with alarm by the people as the first ripples of trouble stirred over the even surface of the river of their lives. If both the young man and the old man were visiting the same hut, they reasoned, perhaps the old man had not died a normal death. They questioned the councillors who knew all secrets.

'Monemapee died just walking on his own feet,' they said reassuringly.

That matter settled, the next challenge came from the two junior brothers, Ntema and Mosemme. If Sebembele were claiming the child, Makobi, as his son, they said, it meant that the young child displaced them in seniority. That they could not allow. The subtle pressure exerted on Sebembele by his junior brothers and the councillors was that he should renounce Rankwana and the child and all would be well. A chief lacked nothing and there were many other women more suitable as wives. Then Sebembele made the second blunder. In a world where women were of no account, he said truthfully:

'The love between Rankwana and I is great.'

This was received with cold disapproval by the councillors.

'If we were you,' they said, 'we would look for a wife somewhere else. A ruler must not be carried away by his emotions. This matter is going to cause disputes among the people.'

They noted that on being given this advice, Sebembele became very quiet, and they left him to his own thoughts, thinking that sooner or later he would come to a decision that agreed with theirs.

In the meanwhile the people quietly split into two camps. The one camp said:

'If he loves her, let him keep her. We all know Rankwana. She is a lovely person, deserving to be the wife of a chief.'

The other camp said:

'He must be mad. A man who is influenced by a woman is no ruler. He is like one who listens to the advice of a child. This story is really bad.'

There was at first no direct challenge to the chieftaincy which Sebembele occupied. But the nature of the surprising dispute, that of his love for a woman and a child, caused it to drag on longer than time would allow. Many evils began to rear their heads like impatient hissing snakes, while Sebembele argued with his own heart or engaged in tender dialogues with his love, Rankwana.

'I don't know what I can do,' Sebembele said, torn between the demands of his position and the strain of a love affair which had been conducted in deep secrecy for many, many months. The very secrecy of the affair seemed to make it shout all the louder for public recognition. At one moment his heart would urge him to renounce the woman and child, but each time he saw Rankwana it abruptly said the opposite. He could come to no decision.

It seemed little enough that he wanted for himself—the companionship of a beautiful woman to whom life had given many other attractive gifts; she was gentle and kind and loving. As soon as Sebembele communicated to her the advice of the councillors, she bowed her head and cried a little.

'If that is what they say, my love,' she said in despair, 'I have no hope left for myself and the child. It were better if we were both dead.'

'Another husband could be chosen for you,' he suggested.

'You doubt my love for you, Sebembele,' she said. 'I would kill myself if I lose you. If you leave me, I would kill myself.'

Her words had meaning for him because he was trapped in the same kind of anguish. It was a terrible pain which seemed to paralyse his movements and thoughts. It filled his mind so completely that he could think of nothing else, day and night. It was like a sickness, this paralysis, and like all ailments it could not be concealed from sight; Sebembele carried it all around with him.

'Our hearts are saying many things about this man,' the councillors said among themselves. They were saying that he was unmanly; that he was unfit to be a ruler; that things were slipping from his hands. Those still sympathetic approached him and said:

'Why are you worrying yourself like this over a woman, Sebembele? There are no limits to the amount of wives a chief may have, but you cannot have that woman and that child.'

And he only replied with a distracted mind: 'I don't know what I can do.'

But things had been set in motion. All the people were astir over events; if a man couldn't make up his mind, other men could make it up for him.

Everything was arranged in secret and on an appointed day Rankwana and the child were forcibly removed back to her father's home. Ever since the controversy had started, her father had been harassed day and night by the councillors as an influence that could help to end it. He had been reduced to a state of agitated muttering to himself by the time she was brought before him. The plan was to set her up with a husband immediately and settle the matter. She was not yet formally married to Sebembele.

'You have put me in great difficulties, my child,' her father said, looking away from her distressed face. 'Women never know their own minds and once this has passed away and you have many children you will wonder what all the fuss was about.'

'Other women may not know their minds . . .' she began, but he stopped her with a raised hand, indicating the husband who had been chosen for her. In all the faces surrounding her there was no sympathy or help, and she quietly allowed herself to be led away to her new home.

When Sebembele arrived in his own yard after a morning of attending to the affairs of the land, he found his brothers, Ntema and Mosemme there.

'Why have you come to visit me?' he asked, with foreboding. 'You never come to visit me. It would seem that we are bitter enemies rather than brothers.'

'You have shaken the whole town with your madness over a woman,' they replied mockingly. 'She is no longer here so you don't have to say any longer "I-don't-know-what-I-can-do". But we still request that you renounce the child, Makobi, in a gathering before all the people, in order that our position is clear. You must say: "That child Makobi is the younger brother of my brothers, Ntema and Mosemme, and not the son of Sebembele who rules".'

Sebembele looked at them for a long moment. It was not hatred he felt but peace at last. His brothers were forcing him to leave the tribe.

'Tell the people that they should all gather together,' he said. 'But what I say to them is my own affair.'

The next morning the people of the whole town saw an amazing sight which stirred their hearts. They saw their ruler walk slowly and unaccompanied through the town. They saw him pause at the yard of Rankwana's father. They saw Sebembele and Rankwana's father walk to the home of her new husband where she had been secreted. They saw Rankwana and Sebembele walk together through the town. Sebembele held the child Makobi in his arms. They saw that they had a ruler who talked with deeds rather than words. They saw that the time had come for them to offer up their individual faces to the face of this ruler. But the people were still in two camps. There was a whole section of the people who did not like this face; it was too out-of-the-way and shocking; it made them very uneasy. Theirs was not a tender, compassionate, and romantic world. And yet in a way it was. The arguments in the other camp which supported Sebembele had flown thick and fast all this time, and they said:

'Ntema and Mosemme are at the bottom of all this trouble. What are they after for they have set a difficult problem before us all? We don't trust them. But why not? They have not yet had time to take anything from us. Perhaps we ought to wait until they do something really bad; at present they are only filled with indignation at the behaviour of Sebembele. But no, we don't trust them. We don't like them. It is Sebembele we love, even though he has shown himself to be a man with a weakness . . .'

That morning, Sebembele completely won over his camp with his extravagant, romantic gesture, but he lost everything else and the rulership of the kingdom of Monemapee.

When all the people had gathered at the meeting place of the town, there were not many arguments left. One by one the councillors stood up and condemned the behaviour of Sebembele. So the two brothers, Ntema and Mosemme won the day. Still working together as one voice, they stood up and asked if their senior brother had any words to say before he left with his people.

'Makobi is my child,' he said.

'Talaote,' they replied, meaning in the language then spoken by the tribe—'all right, you can go'.

And the name Talaote was all they were to retain of their identity as the people of the kingdom of Monemapee. That day, Sebembele and his people packed their belongings on the backs of their cattle and slowly began the journey southwards. They were to leave many ruins behind them and it is said that they lived, on the journey southwards, with many other tribes like the Baphaleng, Bakaa, and Batswapong until they finally settled in the land of the Bamangwato. To this day there is a separate Botalaote ward in the capital village of the Bamangwato, and the people refer to themselves still as the people of Talaote. The old men there keep on giving confused and contradictory accounts of their origins, but they say they lost their place of birth over a woman. They shake their heads and say that women have always caused a lot of trouble in the world. They say that the child of their chief was named, Talaote, to commemorate their expulsion from the kingdom of Monemapee.

FOOTNOTE:
The story is an entirely romanticized and fictionalized version of the history of the Botalaote tribe. Some historical data was given to me by the old men of the tribe, but it was unreliable as their memories had tended to fail them. A re-construction was made therefore in my own imagination; I am also partly indebted to the London Missionary Society's 'Livingstone Tswana Readers', Padiso III, school textbook, for those graphic paragraphs on the harvest thanksgiving ceremony which appear in the story.

B. HEAD.

Heaven is not Closed

All her life Galethebege earnestly believed that her whole heart ought to be
devoted to God, although one catastrophe after another occurred to deflect
her from this path. It was only in the last five years of her life, after her
husband, Ralokae, had died, that she was able to devote her whole mind to
her calling. Then, all her pent-up and suppressed love for God burst forth
and she talked only of Him, day and night—so her grandchildren, solemnly
and with deep awe, informed the mourners at her funeral. All the mourners
present at her hour of passing were utterly convinced that they had watched
a profound and holy event. They talked about it for days afterwards.

Galethebege was well over ninety when she died and not at all afflicted
by crippling ailments like most of the aged. In fact, only two days before
her death had she complained to her grandchildren of a sudden fever and a
lameness in her legs, and she had remained in bed. A quiet, thoughtful
mood fell upon her. On the morning of the second day she had abruptly
demanded that all the relatives be summoned.

'My hour has come,' she said, with lofty dignity.

No one quite believed it, because that whole morning she had sat bolt
upright in bed and talked to all who had gathered, about God—whom she
loved with her whole heart. Then, exactly at noon, she announced once
more that her hour had indeed come and lay down peacefully like one about
to take a short nap. Her last words were:

'I shall rest now because I believe in God.'

Then, a terrible silence filled the hut and seemed to paralyse the mourners
for they all remained immobile for some time; each person present cried
quietly because not one of them had ever witnessed such a magnificent
death before. They only stirred when the old man, Modise, suddenly
observed, with great practicality that Galethebege was not in the correct
position for death. She lay on her side with her right arm thrust out above
her head. She ought to be turned over on her back, with her hands crossed

7

over her chest, he said. A smile flickered over the old man's face as he said this, as though it was just like Galethebege to make such a miscalculation. Why, she knew the hour of her death and everything, then at the last minute forgot the correct sleeping posture for the coffin. Later that evening, as he sat with his children near the outdoor fire for the evening meal, a smile again flickered over his face.

'I am of a mind to think that Galethebege was praying for forgiveness for her sins this morning,' he said slowly. 'It must have been a sin to her to marry Ralokae. He was an unbeliever to the day of his death . . .'

A gust of astonished laughter shook his family out of the solemn mood of mourning that had fallen upon them and they all turned eagerly towards their grandfather, sensing that he had a story to tell.

'As you all know,' the old man said wisely, 'Ralokae was my brother. But none of you present knows the story of Galethebege's life, but I know it . . .'

As the flickering firelight lit up their faces, he told the following story: 'I was never like Ralokae, an unbeliever. But that man, my brother, draws out my heart. He liked to say that we as a tribe would fall into great difficulties if we forget our own customs and laws. Today, his words seem true. There is thieving and adultery going on such as was not possible under Setswana law.'

In the days when they were young, said the old man, Modise, it had become the fashion for all black people to embrace the Gospel. For some, it was the mark of whether they were 'civilised' or not. For some, like Galethebege, it was their whole life. Anyone with eyes to see would have known that Galethebege had been born good; under any custom, whether Setswana custom or Christian custom, she would still have been good. It was this natural goodness of heart that made her so eagerly pursue the word of the Gospel. There was a look on her face, absent, abstracted, as though she needed to share the final secret of life with God who could understand all things. So she was always on her way to church, and in her hours of leisure at home she could be found with her head buried in the Bible. And so her life would have gone on in this quiet and worshipful way, had not a sudden catastrophe occurred in the yard of Ralokae.

Ralokae had been married for nearly a year when his young wife died in childbirth. She died when the crops of the season were being harvested, and for a year Ralokae imposed on himself the traditional restraints and disciplines of boswagadi or mourning for the deceased. A year later, again at the harvest time, he underwent the cleansing ceremony demanded by custom and could once more resume the normal life of a man. It was the unexpectedness of the tragic event and the discipline it imposed on him, that made Ralokae take note of the life of Galethebege. She lived just three yards away from his own yard, and formerly he had barely taken note of her existence; it was too quiet and orderly. But during the year of mourning, it delighted him to hear that gentle and earnest voice of Galethebege informing him that such tragedies 'were the will of God'. As soon as he could, he began courting her. He was young and impatient to be married again and no one could bring back the dead. So a few days after the cleansing ceremony, he made his intentions very clear to her.

'Let us two get together,' he said. 'I am pleased by all your ways.'

Galethebege was all at the same time startled, pleased, and hesitant. She was hesitant because it was well known that Ralokae was an unbeliever; he had not once set foot in church. So she looked at him, begging an apology, and mentioned the matter which was foremost in her mind.

'Ralokae' she said, uncertainly. 'I have set God always before me,' implying by that statement that perhaps he too was seeking a Christian life, like her own. But he only looked at her in a strange way, and said nothing. This matter was to stand like a fearful sword between them but he had set his mind on winning Galethebege as his wife. That was all he was certain of. He turned up in her yard day after day.

'Hullo girlfriend,' he would greet her, enchantingly.

He always wore a black beret perched at a jaunty angle on his head. His walk and manner were gay and jaunty too. He was so exciting as a man that he threw her whole life into turmoil. It was the first time love had come her way and it made the blood pound fiercely through her whole body till she could feel its very throbbing at the tips of her fingers. It turned her thoughts from God a bit, to this new magic life was offering her. The day she agreed to be his wife, that sword quivered like a fearful thing between them. Ralokae said very quietly and firmly: 'I took my first wife according to the old customs. I am going to take my second wife according to the old customs too.'

He could see the protest on her face. She wanted to be married in church according to Christian custom. However, he had his own protest to make. The God might be all right, he explained, but there was something wrong with the people who had brought the word of the Gospel to the land. Their love was enslaving black people and he could not stand it. That was why he was without belief. It was the people he did not trust. They were full of tricks. They were a people who, at the sight of a black man, pointed a finger in the air, looked away into the distance and said impatiently: 'Boy! Will you carry this! Boy! Will you fetch this!' They had brought a new order of things into the land and they made the people cry for love. One never had to cry for love in the customary way of life. Respect was just there for people all the time. That was why he rejected all things foreign.

What could a woman do with a man like that who knew his own mind? She either loved him or she was mad. From that day on, Galethebege knew what she would do. She would do all that Ralokae commanded as a good wife should. But her former life was like a drug. Her footsteps were too accustomed to wearing down the footpath to the church, and there they carried her to the missionary's house which stood just under the shadow of the church.

The missionary was a short, anonymous-looking man who wore glasses. He had been the resident missionary for some time, and like all his fellows he did not particularly like the people. He always complained to his own kind that they were terrible beggars and rather stupid. So when he opened the door and saw Galethebege there his expression, with its raised eyebrows said: 'Well, what do you want now?'

'I am to be married, sir,' Galethebege said politely, after the exchange of greetings.

The missionary smiled: 'Well come in my dear. Let us talk about the arrangements,' he said pleasantly.

He stared at her with polite, professional interest. She was a complete non-entity, a part of the vague black blur which was his congregation—oh, they noticed chiefs and people like that, but not the silent mass of humble and lowly who had an almost weird capacity to creep quietly through life. Her next words brought her sharply into focus.

'The man I am to marry, sir, does not wish to be married in the Christian way. He will only marry under Setswana custom,' she said softly.

They always knew the superficial stories about 'heathen customs' and an expression of disgust crept into his face—sexual malpractices were associated with the traditional marriage ceremony (and shudder!), they draped the stinking intestinal bag of the ox around their necks.

'That we cannot allow!' he said sharply. 'Tell him to come and marry in the Christian way.'

Galethebege started trembling all over. She looked at the missionary in alarm. Ralokae would never agree to this. Her intention in approaching the missionary was to acquire his blessing for the marriage, as though a compromise of tenderness could be made between two traditions opposed to each other. She trembled because it was beyond her station in life to be involved in controversy and protest. The missionary noted the trembling and alarm and his tone softened a bit, but his next words were devastating.

'My dear,' he said persuasively, 'heaven is closed to the unbeliever . . .'

Galethebege stumbled home on shaking legs. It never occurred to her to question such a miserable religion which terrified people with the fate of eternal damnation in hell-fire if they were 'heathens' or sinners. Only Ralokae seemed quite unperturbed by the fate that awaited him. He smiled when Galethebege relayed the words of the missionary to him.

'Girlfriend,' he said, carelessly, 'you can choose what you like, Setswana custom or Christian custom. I have chosen to live my life by Setswana custom.'

Not once in her life had Galethebege's integrity been called into question. She wanted to make the point clear.

'What you mean, Ralokae,' she said firmly, 'is that I must choose you over my life with the church. I have a great love in my heart for you so I choose you. I shall tell the priest about this matter because his command is that I marry in church.'

Even Galethebege was astounded by the harshness of the missionary's attitude. The catastrophe she did not anticipate, was that he abruptly excommunicated her from the Church. She could no longer enter the village church if she married under Setswana custom. It was beyond her to reason that the missionary was the representative of both God and something evil, the mark of 'civilisation'. It was unthinkable that an illiterate and ignorant man could display such contempt for the missionary's civilisation. His rage and hatred were directed at Ralokae, and the only way in which he could inflict punishment was to banish Galethebege from the Church. If it hurt anyone at all, it was only Galethebege. The austere rituals of the Church, the mass, the sermons, the intimate communication in prayer with God—all this had thrilled her heart deeply. But Ralokae also was representative of an ancient stream of holiness that people had lived with before any white man had set foot in the land, and it only needed a small protest to stir up loyalty for the old customs.

The old man, Modise, paused at this point in the telling of his tale but his young listeners remained breathless and silent, eager for the conclusion.

'Today,' he continued, 'it is not a matter of debate because the young care neither way about religion. But in that day, the expulsion of Galethebege from the Church was a matter of debate. It made the people of our village ward think. There was great indignation because both Galethebege and

Ralokae were much respected in the community. People then wanted to know how it was that Ralokae, who was an unbeliever, could have heaven closed to him? A number of people, including all the relatives who officiated at the wedding ceremony, then decided that if heaven was closed to Galethebege and Ralokae it might as well be closed to them too, so they all no longer attended church. On the day of their wedding, we had all our own things. Everyone knows the extent to which the cow was a part of the people's life and customs. We took our clothes from the cow and our food from the cow and it was the symbol of our wealth. So the cow was a holy thing in our lives. The elders then cut the intestinal bag of the cow in two and one portion was placed around the neck of Galethebege and one portion around the neck of Ralokae to indicate the wealth and good luck they would find together in married life. Then the porridge and meat were dished up in our mogopo bowls which we had used from old times. There was much capering and ululating that day because Ralokae had honoured the old customs . . .'

A tender smile once more flickered over the old man's face.

'Galethebege could never forsake the custom in which she had been brought up. All through her married life she would find a corner in which to pray. Sometimes Ralokae would find her so and ask: "What are you doing, Mother?" And she would reply: "I am praying to God." Ralokae would only smile. He did not even know how to pray to the Christian God.'

The old man leaned forward and stirred the dying fire with a partially burnt-out log of wood. His listeners sighed the way people do when they have heard a particularly good story. As they stared at the fire they found themselves debating the matter in their minds, as their elders had done some forty or fifty years ago. Was heaven really closed to the unbeliever, Ralokae? Or had Christian custom been so intolerant of Setswana custom that it could not hear the holiness of Setswana custom? Wasn't there a place in heaven too for Setswana custom? Then the gust of astonished laughter shook them again. Galethebege had been very well-known in the village ward over the past five years for the supreme authority with which she had talked about God. Perhaps her simple and good heart had been terrified that the doors of heaven were indeed closed on Ralokae and she had been trying to open them.

The Village Saint

People were never fooled by façades. They would look quietly and humorously behind the façade at the real person—cheat, liar, pompous condescending sham, and so on—and nod their heads in a certain way until destiny caught up with the decrepit one. The village could be rocked from end to end by scandal; the society itself seemed to cater for massive public humiliations of some of its unfortunate citizens and during those times all one's fanciful, heretical, or venal tendencies would be thoroughly exposed. Despite this acute insight into human nature, the whole village was aghast the day it lost its patron saint, Mma-Mompati. She had had a long reign of twenty-six years, and a fool-proof façade.

Oh, the story was a long one. It was so long and so austere and holy that it was written into the very stones and earth of village life. And so habitual had her own pose of saintliness become to her that on the day her graven image shattered into a thousand fragments, she salvaged some of the pieces and was still seen at the head of the funeral parade or praying for the sick in hospital.

Mma-Mompati and her husband, Rra-Mompati, belonged to the elite of the village. At the time of their marriage, Rra-Mompati held an important position in tribal affairs. It was so important that he lived in a large, whitewashed, colonial-style house with many large rooms. A wide porch, enclosed with mosquito netting, surrounded the whole house. It was to this house that the elders of the tribe retired to discuss top-secret affairs and it was in this house that Mma-Mompati first made her début as the great lady of the town.

Their only son, Mompati, was born a year after marriage into this state of affairs—he was born into the Bamangwato tribe, which, as most people know, was famous or notorious for a history of unexpected explosions and intrigues. The child was welcomed tenderly by his father and named Mompati—my little travelling companion. All three members of the family were spectacular in their own ways, but people tended to forget the former names of the parents—they were simply known as Father of Mompati or Mother of Mompati. The child, Mompati, hardly fulfilled the forecast of his name. Indeed, he travelled side by side with his father for sixteen years, he travelled side by side with his mother for another ten years but when he eventually emerged as a personality in his own right, he became known rather as the warm-hearted, loud-voiced firm defender of all kinds of causes—marriage, morals, child care, religion, and the rights of the poor.

Mompati started his career early in that great white-washed colonial house. Whenever an explosion occurred, and there were many at one stage, the elders of the tribe did not wish the people to know of their secret deliberations and this left the people in an agony of suspense and tension. Some people, under cover of dark, would try to creep onto the wide porch of the house and hold their ears near the window to try and catch only *one* word of the hush-hush talks. A little patrolman soon appeared on stocky, stubby legs with a set, earnest expression who took turn after turn on duty around the porch to keep all eavesdroppers at bay. Seeing Mompati, the eavesdroppers would back away, laughing and shaking their heads in frustration.

'It was no good,' they would report to the people. 'The little policeman was on duty.'

And so life went on in that great house. The tribal intrigues and explosions came; the intrigues and explosions became irrelevant. The great lady of the town, Mma-Mompati, was seen everywhere, She had the close, guarded eyes of one who knows too much and isn't telling. She presided over teas and luncheons in her home, just like any English lady, with polished etiquette and the professional smile of the highborn who don't really give a damn about people or anything. And as though to off-set all the intrigues and underworld deals that went on in her home behind closed doors, Mma-Mompati assiduously cultivated her 'other image' of the holy woman. No villager could die without being buried by Mma-Mompati: she attended the funerals of rich and poor. No one could fall ill without receiving the prayers of Mma-Mompati. Two days a week she set aside for visits to the hospital and in the afternoon, during visiting hours, she made the rounds of the hospital ward, Bible in hand. She would stop at each bed and enquire solicitously:

'And what may ail you, my daughter? And what may ail you, my son?'

At which, of course, the grateful ailing one would break out with a long list of woes. She had a professional smile and a professional frown of concern for everything, just like the priests. But topping it all was the fluidity and ease with which she could pray.

'Oh,' she would say, stricken with sorrow. 'I shall pray for you,' and bending her head in deep concentration she would pray and pray to either God or Jesus for the suffering of the world. Needless to say these gestures were deeply appreciated.

Then one day, without any warning, Rra-Mompati brought his world crashing down around his ears. He just preferred another woman and walked out of the security and prestige of his job and home to live with her. It was one of those scandals that rocked the village from end to end and for a time Rra-Mompati shuffled around shame-faced at his appalling deed. He averted his face so as not to catch the angry looks of the villagers which clearly said: 'Now Rra-Mompati, how could you leave a good woman like Mma-Mompati? She is matchless in her perfection. There is no other woman like her.'

On this tide of indignation Mma-Mompati swept sedately into the divorce court. The whole village memorized her great court oration because she repeated it so often thereafter. It was to God, the Church, the Bible, the Sick, the Poor, the Suffering, the Honour of an Honourable Woman, the Blessings of Holy Matrimony and so on. The court was very impressed by this noble, wronged woman. They ordered that Rra-Mompati, who was rich, settle her handsomely for life, with many cattle. Life in the village became very difficult for Rra-Mompati. People muttered curses at the very sight of him, and as for his new-found lady-love, she dared not show her face. He was also advised by the elders that a man of his low morals could not be in charge of the affairs of the tribe and he ought to look for another job. Rra-Mompati failed to defend himself, except in odd ways. After a long silence he told a sympathetic friend that he was sick of the nonsense of the village and would retire permanently to his cattle-post and live henceforth the life of a cattle-man. He was highly indignant, in an illogical way, at people, for turning against him.

Rra-Mompati was very indignant with his son, Mompati, for turning against him in support of his mother and he clung to these two indignations with a strange stubbornness. Soon after the father had disappeared from the village, he was pursued by Mompati in a heart-breaking attempt at reconciliation. Mompati returned to the village with a shocking story. On approaching his father's cattle-post, he said, his father had walked out of his hut and pointed his hunting gun at him. Then he'd shouted: 'Get away from here! You can support that woman if you like!'

Oh, the Devil had taken Rra-Mompati's soul for good, people said. He would surely burn eternally in hell-fire. Soon after this Mompati became very ill. He lay down for months. He had a terrible weakness and pain all over his body. He developed a fear of any chill or draught. It would end his life and he enveloped himself with warm clothing and blankets in an effort to save his life. Not once did he relate his nervous breakdown to the actions of his father but when he recovered a little he told people very earnestly that he was suffering from 'poor blood'. He kept this ailment as a kind of chronic condition and winter and summer he wrapped himself up warmly against the elements. In summer, the sweltering desert heat of the village reached temperatures of a hundred degrees in the shade. Mompati was wrapped up in two jerseys and an overcoat on such days. One day a per-spiring villager remarked on the heat and looked meaningfully at Mompati's jerseys and coat. Mompati shivered and said: 'I have to protect myself. I must take care of my poor blood.'

Mma-Mompati settled in a little Mother Hubbard house with her son. It was neatly fenced. A water tap appeared in the yard, and vegetables and flower gardens tended by servants sprang up all round the pretty little house. Mompati found a job as a manager of a village store and together they resumed the broken thread of their lives. Mompati was seventeen then and astonishingly like his mother in appearance and behaviour. Mma-Mompati kept to her round of funerals, hospital visits, and church-going and her son built up a public acclaim all his own. Like his mother, he cared about every-one and it was due to this that he managed one of the strangest stores on earth. It was always crowded with people but it often ran completely out of goods. Above the clamour of voices, every now and then rose the deep, booming bass of Mompati, either in a hearty laugh or in stern and forcefully delivered advice to those in conflict or pain. He sat in a corner with piles of accounts and book-work but he could be easily distracted from his work. Every now and then he would look up cheerfully at the approach of a friend but that cheerful smile could, in a split second, turn to a worried frown. He would have one finger on his accounting—it would remain firmly pressed there—and a half an hour might pass in earnest discussion of the friend's latest problem. Suddenly, the bass voice would boom through the shop:

'I say, my friend, if you spare the rod, you spoil the child.'

Shoppers never knew the whole story. It did not matter. It mattered that some living being cared intensely and vividly and gloriously about his fellow men. A slight hush would descend on the shop as the bass swelled out and people would smile to themselves. It swelled out about God who was important and behind all things; it swelled out about the morals of the land which were disintegrating and later, when he married, it swelled out about the virtues of family life. He threw his whole heart into peoples' affairs and then, at the end of the day took all his book-work and accounting home, sitting up until late at night to make up for the hours lost in conversation during the day. Sometimes shoppers humourously queried:

'Mompati, why is it that there is no flour or soap in this shop? I've hunted for these goods for a whole week here and I cannot find them.'

And Mompati would reply: 'That's just what I was praying to God about this morning: "Oh God," I said, "I've forgotten to order the flour and soap again. I beg of you to help me, God, because my memory is so poor." My prayer has been answered my friend, and I expect the flour and soap to be here next week . . .'

This went on for ten years. Both mother and son lived a busy life and people imagined they were two peas in a pod, they seemed so alike in their interests and behaviour. Then Mompati fell in love with Mary Pule, a thin, wilting, willowy dreamy girl with a plaintive, tremulous voice. She had a façade too that concealed a tenacious will. She was so anxious to secure Mompati permanently as a husband that she played a hard game. All during the time he courted her, and it took months, she led him this way and that, with a charming smile. Oh, maybe she loved him. Maybe she did not. She wasn't sure. Mompati was intense about everything, so he was intensely in love. He shared his depressions and elations with his mother. The girl was invited to teas and showered with flattery and teasing until, in her own time, she accepted his proposal. It had nothing to do with either Mompati or his mother. It was her own plan.

A small flat was built in the yard in preparation for Mompati's future married life, and all proceeded well up to a certain point—the month after the marriage. Then Mma-Mompati began to undo herself. Throughout the ten years she had lived with her son, she had played a little game. Mompati used to bring his pay-packet home intact but she wanted him to buy her just a teeny-weeny something—a pair of stockings, a bottle of scent, a little handkerchief or a new dress. It just pleased her, she said, that her son cared about his mother. So she always extracted a teeny bit for her share and handed him the rest. She soon informed her daughter-in-law of this procedure and like all powerful personalities, she secretly despised the weak, wilting, plaintive little wretch her son had married. She needed to dominate and shove the wretch around. So at the end of that month, she over-stepped the mark. She opened the pay-packet as usual and suddenly needed an enormous amount of things all at once—a pair of shoes, a new dress, and a necklace.

What she handed over to her son could barely keep him and his wife in food for a week. She could not follow them into the privacy of their home, but unconsciously her vampire teeth were bared for battle. She noted that her daughter-in-law often looked gloomy and depressed in the ensuing days; her son was cold and reserved. She attacked the daughter-in-law with brittle smiles:

'Well, what's wrong with you, my child? Can't you greet an old person in a cheerful way?'

'There's nothing wrong, mother,' the girl replied, with a painful smile.

At the end of the next month, Mompati walked straight to his own flat and handed his pay-packet intact to his wife, ate a good supper, and fell into a sound sleep after many nights of worry and anguish. The following morning he left for work without even a glance at his mother's home. Then the storm burst. The pose of God and Jesus were blown to the winds and the demented vampire behind it was too terrible to behold. She descended on her daughter-in-law like a fury.

'You have done this to my son!' she snarled. 'You have turned him against me! His duty is to respect me and honour me and you cannot take it away from me! You see that water tap? You shall not draw any more water from it while you are in this yard! Go and draw water at the village tap in future!'

And so the whole village became involved in the spectacle. They stopped and blinked their eyes as they saw the newly-wed Mary carrying a water bucket a mile away from her own home to the village water taps.

'Mary,' they asked curiously, 'why is it you have to draw water here like everyone else when your mother-in-law has a water tap in her yard?'

Mary talked freely and at great length—a long weepy story of misery and torture. And people said: 'Well, we can't believe that a good woman like Mma-Mompati could be so harsh to her own child,' and they shook their heads in amazement at this thunderbolt. That was the end of Mma-Mompati. No one ever believed in her again or her God or Jesus Christ but she still buried the dead and prayed for the sick.

Her son, Mompati, set up home in a far-off part of the village. He never discussed the abrupt break with his mother to whom he had once been so overwhelmingly devoted, but one day his voice suddenly boomed out through the store in reply to some request by a friend:

'I'm sorry,' he said. 'I never do anything without first consulting my wife . . .'

Jacob: The Story of a Faith-Healing Priest

The quiet, sleepy village of Makaleng was about thirty miles from a big railway station in Northern Botswana. Makaleng village was quiet and sleepy because the people were fat and well-fed. Envious visitors to the village often exclaimed that there must be something wrong with the sky overhead, because whilst the rest of the country was smitten by drought year after year, Makaleng village never failed to receive its yearly quota of twenty-two inches of rain. Whenever people stood in groups and shook their heads sadly about another of those summers of no rain and no crops, someone would always interrupt to say:

'But I've just come from Makaleng village. The people there are eating water-melon and fresh green mealies. And from their lands they are about to harvest bags and bags of corn.'

Thus, Makaleng was one of those far-away wonders of the world which people sometimes visited but never thought of inhabiting. It never occurred to people perishing of drought and hunger to rush there in droves, settle there, and produce their crops and raise their cattle in ease and comfort. As it was, good fortune was added to good fortune in Makaleng. The village had a small population of about five hundred people and a big, broad sandy river cut its way through the central part of the village. In the summer this river flowed in torrents of muddy water, and in winter gigantic pools of water shimmered like mercury in the pot-holes of its sandy bed.

The summer grass of Makaleng was a miracle too. It shot seven feet high into the sky like a thick, dense jungle which terrified the small boys who herded the cattle. The small boys had a secret joke among themselves about the summer grass of Makaleng. They never set foot in it. Early each morning they would stand at its perimeter and drive the cattle into this dark jungle of stalks and leaves to graze. Once the last swishing tail had disappeared, they would retreat as far as possible, hugging their arms around their bony chests so afraid were they of the terror that lived all summer long in the dense grass. For some hours a deep silence would reign over the grazing area; then all of a sudden, the agonized bellows of the cattle and their mad, stampeding feet would send the birds into the air with startled shrieks and make the cattleboys jump for their sticks. A ferocious vampire-fly bred in the long grass and pierced its deep, sharp mouth-parts into the skin of either man or beast to suck up the blood. The pain caused by its sting was excruciating. Yet the cattle never seemed to learn. For once they had stampeded out of the grass and had had the flies beaten off them by the cattle-boys, they allowed themselves to be driven back again into this terrible grazing area. And that's how the cattle were grazed all summer. Maybe cattle-grazing in this manner was a hard job, but if so only the small boys who herded the cattle knew it to be so and maybe by sunset, when they herded the cattle home, they had temporarily forgotten the vampire-fly. They laughed and joked among themselves, and as soon as they entered their yards, they started fights with their sisters.

It's not certain what the authorities thought about the village of Makaleng and its good twenty-two inches of rain, or whether the area was suited to agricultural development or not. Someone had muttered something about the soil; it became too easily waterlogged. Nor did the ordinary people of the country visit Makaleng because the people there were eating fresh green mealies in a drought year. Oh no, Makaleng village was famous in the hearts of ordinary people because it had two prophets.

The one prophet, Jacob, lived on the sunrise side of the village. The other prophet, Lebojang, lived on the sunset side. Prophet Jacob was very poor and lived in a mud hut. He walked around with no shoes. Prophet Lebojang was very rich. He lived in a great mansion and drove around in a very posh car.

It was not the habit of Prophet Lebojang to notice the existence of Prophet Jacob, except that on one occasion Prophet Jacob had entered his yard on the death of a relative. But Prophet Jacob attended all funerals from the sympathy and kindness of his heart; he was unperturbed by the cold reception given him by Lebojang and his followers, and the fact that he was overlooked when plates of food were handed round. Much more terrible things had Lebojang done to him on his arrival in Makaleng. There was a time when lightning used to strike the hut of Prophet Jacob, though there was not a cloud in the sky. There was a time when an enormous hissing snake would suddenly manifest itself in the hut of Prophet Jacob, but neither lightning, nor snakes, nor poisoned food and water could take the life of Prophet Jacob. At first, Prophet Jacob had wanted to flee the hatred of Prophet Lebojang, but one night when the persecution and torture had reached its peak, he heard, so he told two close friends, the Voice of his God in the silence of his hut. It said:

'Haven't I always prepared a table for you in the presence of your enemies? Then why don't you trust me to take care of you?'

And that was enough for Prophet Jacob. He no longer feared to stay in Makaleng. It was never quite clear to those who loved Prophet Jacob just who his God was. At times he would refer to him as Jesus. At times his God, in moments of inspiration, appeared to be the width and depth of his own experience and suffering. This he in turn called the Voice which had come to him at all the turning points of his life, forcing him into strange and incomprehensible acts.

There was a time when Prophet Jacob had been as rich a man as Prophet Lebojang. He had been the owner of a store in the big railway village thirty miles from Makaleng. He had had a car, a beautiful wife who loved beautiful clothes, and two pretty daughters. To enable him to give his wife all that she desired, Jacob had even established a big beer-brewing business from which he earned huge profits. After twelve years of this rich and sumptuous living, during which time Jacob drank heavily and lived in the roar of prosperity, a bolt from the blue turned him into a man of rags and tatters overnight. It happened like this: one week his wife had a sudden desire to visit relatives living in another part of the country. She took the two small girls with her and Jacob was left alone. The night of the day of his wife's departure he retired early. At about midnight there was a thunderous, crashing sound at the door. Jacob sprang awake and found his bedroom filled with thieves. Some of the thieves held him down while his hands were tied behind his back and his mouth gagged. As he lay helpless on the floor, the thieves quietly and calmly removed every piece of furniture and clothing from the house. They had already completely emptied the store. All he had left was a few hundred rands in the bank, and he lay there weeping in the darkness. In this darkness and silence he heard the Voice of his God.

'Jacob,' it said quietly, 'why have you forgotten me? It is I who have brought this trouble on you so that you may do my work. From now on you shall only have your daily bread.'

Even though he strained his eyes in the darkness, hoping to get some glimpse of a form which uttered these words, he could see no one. But the words burned into his mind like fire. Not for one moment did he doubt that it was the Voice of his God. And that was enough for Jacob. Amazed neighbours found him the next morning still trussed up and gagged, lying on the floor of his bedroom in the ransacked house behind the ransacked store.

'You must call the police at once,' they said. 'The sooner you report a burglary, the sooner the police will catch up with the thieves.'

But Jacob only stared back at them absent-mindedly. His mind had withdrawn itself from preoccupations with business. Besides, how could he explain the truth to them? How could he tell them he had heard a Voice in the night and that the Voice had claimed responsibility for the thefts? Hadn't the Voice said so? It wasn't a matter that could be mentioned to the police either. It was better to remain silent than to tell the truth. The neighbours watching him remain silent and unmoving on the floor, clucked, clucked sympathetically and shook their heads. Among themselves they said:

'This sudden trouble has unhinged the mind of our friend, Jacob. Look, he can't utter a word.'

Some of the women began to weep loudly. They could not forget the days of starvation in their own homes and the way in which Jacob had never turned a hungry child away from his door. Jacob was widely commended as a good man because of his generosity, and their weeping was meant to be an unspoken rebuke to God. Why did he strike down the good man, always? They wept this way when any of their children died and unconsciously created legends about their saintliness.

Two weeks later, Jacob's wife returned to this changed situation. As she breezed into the house with her high-heeled shoes and big, wide, red-painted mouth, it seemed to Jacob that he was seeing the type of woman he had married for the first time. He said to himself: 'I shall tell her the truth. If she is really my wife, she will give up these ways and join me in the work I have to do.'

'Darling,' she gushed, flinging off a brilliant red turban and kicking off her shoes. 'I've already heard the news. All up and down the line people are talking of nothing else. They even say it has unsettled your mind. I said: "Bosh! we'll make it up in no time." And so here I am, all ready to give it a go.'

She paused and looked at him with a brilliant smile. He looked back at her, almost choked with fear. Had they really not communicated with each other throughout these twelve years of married life? Her mood was so foreign, as though their lives had never flowed together. But what really choked him was his own nature which had constantly sought security; he had never loved any other woman because of this desire for emotional security. Now he was to lose this too. Still, he said the fatal words, so gravely and so finally:

'We are not going back to the old ways of trading in liquor,' he said. 'I have to do the work of the Lord.'

She laughed, ha! ha! ha! in a gay and brittle way. Life had never had any depth for her. She was always in such a rush. She was also a woman of practical common sense with no whims or fancies.

'You aren't serious darling?' she said, with raised eyebrows.

'I am,' he said.

'But who is this Lord?' she said. 'No one has ever seen him. There's nothing we Africans have but the Lord. We sit down and pray to the Lord all the time but he doesn't bring us one ounce of sugar. It would be a different thing if he came down to earth and we could see him. But no one takes the Lord seriously, darling. He doesn't come down.'

'You may say so,' Jacob replied, 'but I have heard the Voice of the Lord and I cannot disobey it.'

He had in his hand the last R10.000 he had withdrawn from the bank. He handed it to his wife, stood up, and walked out of the empty house not looking back once, not even at his two wide-eyed little girls. The Voice of the Lord had told him to go to Makaleng.

* * *

It was not the first time Jacob had tasted wealth and had wealth removed from him, overnight. He was born into wealth. His father was a German who had come to Botswana with an eye to the cattle speculating business. Many a man had reached near millionaire-hood on cattle speculating because it was quick, easy money. The German had married a Motswana woman and established a cattle ranch, mostly used as a transit farm for fattening all the lean cattle he bought as a speculation from the local people. The ranch was not many miles from the village of Makaleng and it did not take him many months to organise his cattle business and have thousands of rands in the bank. His wife also bore him twins, two boys—one of whom she named Jacob, and the other Isaac, these names having been obtained from her studies of the Bible. If questioned about this part of his life, Jacob cannot remember it too well. He vaguely remembers wearing shoes and being well clothed and sleeping in a bed with sheets. But of his father and mother he has little recollection. One day, not long after Jacob and Isaac had turned six years old, his father and mother took a trip by car into the village of Makaleng. As they were crossing the narrow bridge which spanned the broad river in a heavy downpour, the car skidded and went over the edge into the muddy torrent below. Both were killed.

As from nowhere, along came an uncle, the brother of Jacob's mother, weeping bitter tears over the death of his sister. He approached a certain chief of Makaleng and offered to act as guardian of the two boys until they were old enough to inherit their father's wealth. What happened subsequently has often made people say that the then chief of Makaleng village had a share in the robbery of the children's inheritance. It was his duty to see that the guardianship of the children was conducted in an honourable way yet, to the many aghast comments from the people of Makaleng, he only turned a deaf ear. The uncle, the brother of Jacob's mother, became overnight the richest man in Makaleng. His brood of twelve children walked about in shoes and socks. He acquired a brick house and a car and was seen to wave about thick wads of money in the hotel bar of the big railway village. On the other hand, his sister's children, Jacob and Isaac, who now lived with him, were seen to walk about the village without shoes, dressed in the discarded rags and tatters of their uncle's children. What little was left after the wholesale slaughter and sale of the fifty-thousand cattle was given to the two small boys, Jacob and Isaac, to herd in the traditional way in the vampire-fly, grazing-ground of Makaleng. Not once after that did the uncle's children have to soil their hands with work. They had acquired two slaves.

Those who are born to suffer, experience suffering to its abysmal depths. The damage to the two children did not stop at the expropriation of their inheritance. It was now claimed by the uncle and all the relatives that since the children were not pure Batswana by birth, they were therefore of an inferior species. They were fed according to their status. They were given plain porridge with salt and water at every meal, day in and day out, year in and year out. Their sleeping quarters were a ramshackle hut at the bottom of their uncle's yard. They slept on pieces of sacking and lived out their whole lives in that dog house.

Jacob is old now. He relates these experiences of his childhood without bitterness. He will also tell you that his uncle, as though prompted by a subconscious guilt, sent him and his brother to the night school of Makaleng village together with all the small cattle-herding boys who could not attend school during the day. He even remembers the way they were taught to sing the alphabet and clap their hands.

There is a point in his story when you begin to doubt Jacob's sanity and that of his God. Somehow you don't doubt his adult experiences and his conversations with God, but you doubt cruelty and stress placed on a young and helpless child. It's when he tells you about what happened when he was twelve years old that a bad light is thrown on Jacob's God. At this time Jacob's twin brother Isaac died, worn out by the poor diet and hard labour. A deep and terrifying loneliness possessed the heart of the small boy who was left behind that night. He had lost the only living being who had shared some love with him in a world peopled by monsters. There is much said about the love and sharing to be found within tribal societies and much of this is true—but true too is Jacob's uncle. Any child trapped in this cycle of cruelty can find no way out except to cry lonely, hot tears in the dark night.

At this point, says Jacob, while he lay alone in his broken-down hut, weeping, he first heard the Voice of his God.

'Jacob,' it said, 'One day I shall call you to do my work. All the suffering you endure now is but a preparation for the work you have to do.'

Jacob sat up startled, dashing the tears from his eyes. At that time also his eyes searched for a presence or form in the room but there was nothing, only the strong impression of having heard a Voice. You lean forward eagerly towards the now old man; his God seems very dubious, so you ask: Did he bring a little piece of meat on the morrow to eat with that dreadful porridge? Did he change the world and give a jersey to a little boy shivering in tattered clothes? To all your questions Jacob responds with a look of baffled surprise. It has not occurred to him to ask his God for anything all these long long years. He has been too busy fulfilling the orders and strange commands of that Voice. It didn't seem as though Jacob's God wanted him to have anything for himself, even when he was little. No meat came. No jersey. It makes you feel something is wrong because even in old age Jacob hasn't got shoes. It makes you feel like breaking down and weeping because even in old age Jacob hasn't got shoes. So you say, almost violently: Does he love you this God? Why do you let him disrupt your life like that?

Jacob keeps silent a moment sorting this out. Then he tells you that every time he heard that Voice a great peace would fill his heart; that peace gave him the courage to do whatever the Voice requested of him. To an outsider there never seemed to be much coherence in what was going on between Jacob and his God. But the way in which he expressed this relationship in deeds arrested the attention. Everything about him was very beautiful and simple and deeply sincere. He had too, one of the oddest churches in the whole wide world.

*   *   *

On his arrival in the village of Makaleng after parting company from his wife, Jacob set about constructing a mud hut which was to be used both as accommodation for himself and his church. His uncle and the chief of Makaleng who had stolen the inheritance of himself and his brother, were long since dead. At the time of his uncle's death the relatives had squabbled and torn each other to pieces over what remained of the wealth which was not theirs. These relatives lived on the sunset side of the village and were the followers of Prophet Lebojang. The relatives, like Prophet Lebojang, affected in public not to be aware of the sudden and unexpected return of Jacob. He had been away from the village for almost fourteen years, having walked out of his uncle's home as soon as he realised that he could stand on his own two feet and earn his living. But secretly, like all thieves, they were at first intensely interested in the activities of Jacob on the sunrise side of the village, fearing that he might still start a commotion about his stolen inheritance. They also knew about all the black magic spells Prophet Lebojang was casting on Prophet Jacob. No one quite knew why Prophet Lebojang did not have Prophet Jacob killed outright once the black magic powers had failed to destroy him. Some think that the Voice of Prophet Jacob's God might have spoken to Prophet Lebojang and told him under no circumstances to harm Prophet Jacob. This was a rumour in the village, said to have issued from the mouth of Prophet Lebojang.

But the activities of Prophet Jacob on the sunrise side of the village soon had the relatives and Prophet Lebojang rolling on the ground with laughter. After he had completed his hut, Prophet Jacob purchased for himself some cheap material which he shaped into a priestly cloak and in one corner pinned a small cross. He next made a wooden table and carved three wooden candlesticks. Those candlesticks he placed on the table and always, when he wanted to pray, he placed a jug of fresh, clean water near the candlesticks. Curious people would often question him about the water jug and he would reply simply that his God had ordered him to put the water there. After each session of prayer, he was to put the water in bottles and then give it freely to anyone who suffered from ailments or sorrow. His God had assured him that the blessed water would remove all people's troubles.

It took great simplicity of heart to approach a church such as the one conducted by Prophet Jacob. Prophet Jacob had no shoes, so he conducted his services in his bare feet. Many, many strange churches, variants on the Christian religion, exist in Botswana but they all have a bit of glitter and dash. They have funds behind them. Sometimes, like Prophet Lebojang, they put both God and the Devil on the same altar for many years and nothing happens except a great increase in wealth. In contrast to all of them, Prophet Jacob only had the Voice of his God whom he obeyed. From this Voice he received the strictest orders about how to conduct himself. He was never, never under any circumstances to canvass for membership. People would be sent to him. Also, the bare minimum for his daily bread would be given him and this he must break in half and share with whomsoever should step in the door. From these commands Prophet Jacob never deviated one inch.

The next surprise Jacob received was the type of congregation sent to him by his God. One afternoon, towards sunset, as Jacob sat in the silence of his hut, the door was slowly pushed open and six small black heads peered cautiously in.

'We have come to the church, Maruti*' the children said.

Jacob leapt to his feet in great joy and hastened to put on his cloak. The words of the children corresponded to a dream he had had. In the dream he had sung a song. It went like this:

> *Look, I shall be coming again on clouds of glory,*
> *When you see me children,*
> *You must say: Dumelang! Allelujah!*

The song had a very gay rhythm. The little girls got carried away by it, their skirts swishing up and down as they kept time to the beat by clapping their hands vigorously. From that day onwards there was a never-ending bustle of activity in the yard of Jacob, and these activities spread themselves throughout the whole of the sunrise side of the village. The children constantly brought him information of someone ailing there, someone ailing here, and soon it became a not uncommon sight to see Jacob trailing behind a group of children, all singing and making their way to a hut to help someone in sorrow. In all cases the sorrow or ailments would be removed and people would quietly rise up and go about their daily business.

After the first reaction of surprised amusement, no one paid much attention to the church of Jacob because of his poverty and because his congregation was composed entirely of children. No adults joined the church, though through the efforts of the children many of them received a blessing from Jacob's God. A few would approach Jacob wistfully and ask to become members of his church, but he would always reply:

'Please first go to your Maruti and ask his permission.'

*Maruti: a priest.

This permission was never granted. Yet Jacob's reputation spread quietly and persistently; people pointed out his goodness to like-minded people. Thus, when the lorry brought visitors to Makaleng, half the people made their way to the hut of Jacob and half to the mansion of Lebojang. It was almost as though there were no meeting place between the people who went to Jacob and the people who went to Lebojang. Lebojang's relationship with people was that of a businessman. You paid your money and that was that.

If you dressed well and looked rich, a servant would immediately approach you and lead you into Lebojang's plush lounge. There you would be constantly plied with all the good things from Lebojang's pantry until he was free to interview you. If you were in rags and tatters, you sat out all day in the yard and, the interview being over, you would then wander about the village in search of provisions. Lebojang enriched himself from rich and poor alike but he only gave the good things in his pantry to those who had the least need of them. But whether rich or poor, all came to Lebojang for the same purpose—to make use of his stunning powers.

A woman would travel many miles to report to Lebojang that for a long time she had concealed a purse of money under her mattress. One day she had found the purse of money removed and it had been impossible to trace the thief. Lebojang would keep silent awhile, then fix his penetrating eyes on the woman.

'Do you have a friend named Bontle?' he would ask. And the amazed woman would merely nod her head.

'Well,' Lebojang would say. 'It is she who stole your purse on the 25th of February.'

Or again, a woman would say that she had no end of trouble from her husband, who had suddenly taken to drinking heavily. And Lebojang would say:

'Does he have a friend named Toto . . .? Well, this Toto has one aim in mind and that is to take you as his sweetheart. Therefore he leads your husband to drink.'

Such was the power of Lebojang; he would come out with names and dates and prophecies. His charges for these services were very high. It did not matter to him that people were secretly poisoned or driven mad by his prophecies; he simply took his money and that was that. But at least these prophecies of names and dates could bear the light of day. Once his other deeds became known people were to ponder deeply on the nature of evil.

The other half of the lorry-load of visitors to Makaleng had no tales of lost purses or drunken husbands but a terrible anguish of heart. They said to Jacob:

'I have so many troubles. I don't know how to sort them out.'

The practical issues were never discussed. A man in that gathering would have no work for a year and his family would be destitute. After seeing Jacob and participating in the worship of his church, the man would strike a job in two or three days; not anything spectacular, but his poverty would be eased. There was something else too that developed in a quite natural way—an exchange of gifts system. No one ever left Jacob's hut without a parcel. Many grateful seekers of help brought gifts to Jacob; a bag of corn, a bag of sugar, a box of eggs, and so on. These gifts in turn filled many destitute people with good things so that they did not leave Jacob's home hungry. Then too, the church really belonged to the children. They would come in towards the close of day, and the adults would sit to one side as respectful spectators while Jacob and the children conversed with the Lord. No one seemed to question the uniqueness of this, how it was possible for children at the age when their teeth fall out, to turn up promptly at sunset for sermons. Not that they comprehended anything, not even Jacob's simple sermons.

So, in this way, following their two strange occupations, a routine and ritual established itself around the lives of the prophets of Makaleng. Prophet Lebojang increased in wealth, until it was said at the time he met his doom that he was a near-millionaire. Prophet Jacob increased only in his love for the Lord. Seemingly, in gratitude for this, the Lord arranged one more turning point in the life of Prophet Jacob. After many years of living alone, the Lord sent him a wife named Johannah.

* * *

Johannah was a tall, striking handsome woman with a beautifully carved mouth around which a faint smile always lingered. She also had a thick cluster of eyelashes around her pitch black eyes. These two striking features had brought her lots of trouble. She was the sort of woman men would look at twice. Less attractive women were more in tune with the feeling of the times; there was no such thing as marriage left. Johannah had always received proposals of marriage and produced four children always with a view to marrying their fathers, but at the critical moment, the man simply disappeared.

For some years Johannah lived in the yard of her elder brother, who was married. Because of her position as an unmarried woman with children, she assumed the major responsibilities of running the home; washing, cooking for the family and mending the clothes of her brother's children as well as her own. Her brother's wife never soiled her hands with work; either she lay in bed until eleven o'clock in the morning or stood up, dressed herself in smart clothes and spent the day visiting relatives and friends. At least, Johannah reasoned, there was no need for her brother to employ a servant for his fancy wife. Johannah was careful to see that there was no waste in food and other household expenses. In spite of all the services she offered, her brother's manner abruptly changed towards her. He was often angry and impatient with his sister because he was nagged by his wife who had said to him:

'Two of Johannah's children have now reached school-going age. Are you going to foot the bill?'

Thus it was that Johannah found herself confronted by a family conference. Relatives gathered in the yard and to them Johannah's brother put his complaint; he could not afford to support all Johannah's children as well as his own. They spent some time discussing her misdeeds with rising wrath, flinging around such terms as harlot and loose woman who took her sins lightly. Johannah listened to it all with an amused smile, especially her sister-in-law's loud, irate tone. Once Johannah was no longer in the yard would she do all the housework? At last Johannah was allowed to speak. She raised her head proudly and quoted an old proverb:

'I agree with all that has been said about me,' she said. 'But I am a real woman and as the saying goes the children of a real woman do not get lean or die.'

Johannah spent many days wandering hither and thither in search of employment but without success. It was during her wanderings from home to home for possible employment as a house servant that she was told about the Prophet Jacob of Makaleng village who had brought work and comfort to the hearts of many people. One morning before dawn she set out on foot to the village of Makaleng, arriving there about mid-morning.

Like all the visitors to Prophet Jacob, she did not notice his poverty nor the simplicity of his church but right away began confiding the troubles and disappointments of her life. Now and then she would cry a little as she recalled one promise of marriage after another and then the stress of being left alone with fatherless children. She cried in such a peculiar way that even Jacob, who was concentrating his mind on her tale of sorrow, diverted his attention to her tears. They kept welling up in abrupt little bundles which were then caught in the thick cluster of her eyelashes and deposited neatly into her lap. Not one splash soiled the smooth curved surface of her cheek-bones. They were very much an expression of the concentrated emotional intensity of the woman, as though, like her tears, she only saw one thing at a time, in the immediate present, and could not be troubled much about the past. He noted that it was only on actually recalling a disillusionment in words that an abrupt bundle of tears would appear; everything about her was open and straight-forward.

'I have come to see that the faults are all mine,' she said. 'Each time it was I who believed that the father of my child would marry me. I have paid heavily for this error of judgement. But the saying is still there: the children of a real woman cannot fall into the fire.'

Then she lapsed into an abrupt waiting silence keeping her pretty eyes in a steadfast gaze on her lap. Jacob also hesitated. She was the only visitor of the day and she had arrived early. He never said prayers for visitors without the children as they were now an inextricable part of his life. Perhaps the woman would like to prepare some food for herself. She looked extremely hungry.

'Yes indeed,' he said, slowly. 'There are many good sayings in the world. There is the saying that the foot cannot always find its way home. It may be that I should pass your village one day and be afflicted by hunger. You would soon rush to the cooking pot to prepare something for me. Therefore I am paying you for this kindness before it is done. In the corner you will find a bag of corn and next to that a dish of meat. Prepare some food and eat.'

A brief expression of pleased surprise flitted across the woman's face. She arose in one neat self-contained movement and set about to do as he had ordered with a grave, absorbed manner.

'So it's true,' she thought, as she dipped into the bag of corn. 'The man's goodness is expressed in deeds as well as words. How lucky for me that I took this journey. My sorrows are taken away from me this very minute.'

She had far to go on the return journey and without much waste of time Jacob sent a message to the children so that as soon as she had eaten she might receive the prayers and blessed water. In the twinkling of an eye the yard was filled from all directions with rushing feet. Johannah paused in the act of stirring the porridge to stare at the children in amazement. So this was true too; the Prophet kept a church of children. The woman who had told her this had merely shrugged and smiled. Most curious people had, out of a profound respect for Prophet Jacob, refrained from questioning him about this matter.

'I shall certainly bring my children to this church,' Johannah thought to herself. 'There is only goodness here.'

An hour later Johannah was on her way home with a swift, light step. It seemed as though a soft wind blew her home. On her head she carried a quantity of corn for herself and her children and some eggs, sugar, and tea. In her heart she carried a vivid memory of the children's singing.

'How lucky I am,' she thought. 'How wonderful this day has been.'

Alone that night in his hut Jacob found that a wandering mood possessed him. It was always the hour when his soul had soared in peace and freedom, detached from the cares of the day. But on this night it remained firmly on the earth, amusing and entertaining itself with trifles. At first it said:

'Oh, so people cry in all kinds of different ways. Some cry as though they are spitting tears out onto the dry ground.'

Then he would catch himself at this trifling amusement and mutter aloud:

'But I am in old age now. I must be fifty-five,' and he would sigh heavily thinking of his creeping old age. Then the game would start again:

'Porridge is always porridge but some people are better at cooking it than others . . .'

This went on for some time and Jacob was unaware that he was actually smiling to himself. This state of affairs was suddenly interrupted by the Voice of his God sounding loudly and clearly in his ears. It said:

'You are a very foolish man Jacob. How could you let your future wife depart so quickly?'

Being somewhat caught off-balance, for the first time Jacob replied to his God. He said:

'But I am already in old age. She looks about twenty-nine.'

And he turned with a startled expression and stared over his shoulder. But there was no further sound except . . . except an impression of soft laughter. Feeling shaken and confused, Jacob stood up and prepared his blankets on the floor.

* * *

A month went by and then one Sunday morning Johannah arrived once again with the early morning lorry-load of visitors to Makaleng, this time bringing her four children with her. She looked very smart in a new cotton frock and brand new low-heeled shoes. Just a day after she had paid her first visit to Prophet Jacob, she had found a job as a cook and housekeeper for a wealthy person for R10.00 a month. Somehow Prophet Jacob had already known in his heart of her coming, but since the other visitors who also crowded into his yard did not know this secret of his heart there was no one to point out that Prophet Jacob pointedly omitted to gaze in the direction of

Johannah. But there was an intense joy in his heart and a glow like a candle flame in his eyes. The joy in the heart of Prophet Jacob soon affected everyone. A surprise feast was arranged on the spur of the moment. Someone suddenly walked out and bought a goat; another rice, and another some vegetables for salad while the women ran about making preparations for the feast. The children also appeared with their freshly scrubbed faces and clean Sunday clothes and sat among the guests clapping their hands and singing the songs taught to them by Jacob. The villagers of Makaleng were amazed. Never had they heard such a commotion issue from the yard of Prophet Jacob.

'Perhaps Prophet Jacob is holding a marriage feast,' they said. 'Perhaps one of his visitors is getting married.'

And they hastened to wash and make their way to the yard of Prophet Jacob. But no bride and groom were in evidence. There was only joy. Not even prayers were said that day, nor was anyone given the blessed water. Each one was blessed by the joy in his own heart. By sunset, when the lorry turned up to take the visitors back to their own villages, no one wanted to leave. At last the lorry driver had to get out of his lorry and scold the people.

'Look here, people,' he shouted, 'no one pays me for overtime. I have to get back to my wife and children.'

With many wistful, lingering glances, the visitors slowly climbed into the lorry. They kept on repeating to themselves that they would surely visit Prophet Jacob the following Sunday. Since Prophet Jacob was so foolhardy as to omit gazing in any direction that might contain the presence of Johannah, he failed to see that she was not present among the visitors who climbed onto the lorry. But he stood for a long while gazing after it until the flaming red sun dropped down behind the flat horizon. The darkness and gloom that swept down on his heart was like the sudden descent of the black night on Makaleng. He sighed heavily and slowly shuffled towards his lonely hut. It was a good thing for Prophet Jacob that he had a strong heart, for as he pushed open the door of his hut the flaming sun reversed itself and shone again like a dazzling light in the gloom. There was Johannah seated on the floor with her children. Prophet Jacob could not utter a word. He stood for a long while at the door like one stunned. Johannah cried many bundles of neat tears because she could not account for her actions, only that it seemed like her death to climb into the lorry and go away. But, being fearful of this silence, she said painfully:

'You must forgive me. I am so happy here.'

Imagine the amazement of the villagers of Makaleng! That following Monday morning they had to rub their eyes in disbelief and doubt their sanity, for there was Prophet Jacob in his yard with a woman constructing a mud hut. Prophet Jacob had been celebate for so long that they had ceased to regard him as a normal man. Some of the scandal-mongers of the village, hoping to get the full details of this unexpected development, immediately picked up their hoes and dishes and made their way to the yard of Prophet Jacob to help in the construction of the hut. By midday the walls were complete and Prophet Jacob had already set up the framework for the thatched roof. The scandal-mongers were entertained that afternoon by all the women of the village.

'It's true,' they said. 'Prophet Jacob has acquired a new wife.'

Once the impact of it struck their sense of humour, they began to roll on the ground, laughing till the tears poured out of their eyes. In this manner it became an accepted fact that Johannah was the legal wife of Prophet Jacob.

As for Jacob, a whole new world of learning and living opened up for him. He soon found that his home was run peacefully with clockwork precision, by a woman full of the traditions and customs of the country. Jacob had no full knowledge of these customs as his upbringing had been that of an outcast living apart from the household and it was as though he was transported back into a childhood he might have had had his mother lived. His first wife had been a very different type of woman from Johannah, very modern and daring and very de-tribalised. If there were such things as customs which governed the behaviour of children and adults, she knew nothing about this. Now, from Johannah, he was to learn that there were strict, hard-and-fast laws, governing the conduct of family life. In spite of Johannah having produced so many fatherless children, she had indoctrinated them all with the customs of her own childhood so that they were among the most disciplined children on earth. It was an easy, almost effortless act for the children to accept Jacob as their father because according to custom all adult people were regarded as the mothers and fathers of all children.

Jacob was amazed to note how nothing was ever out of place in his home, in spite of its having been invaded so suddenly by so many children. If a guest arrived and was served tea, it would not be long before one of the children appeared and removed the forgotten tea-tray from the floor. Then the cups and pots would be immediately rinsed out and stacked neatly away. There was always a quiet hustle and bustle to and fro. There were always chores for the little girls and boys. There was always wood and water to fetch, corn to stamp and floors to sweep, and never for a moment did the children sit idle during the daylight. Thinking of the hardship of his own childhood when he had longed to play, Jacob one day questioned his wife:

'Why so much work for the children?' he asked. 'When do they have time to play?'

She kept silent a while, staring steadfastly into her lap. Then she said, smiling faintly:

'We must teach the children the real things, husband. Is life play? No, it is hardship. Therefore it's better for the children to learn this lesson while young so that they will stand up to the hardship.'

There seemed to be much sense in her reasoning, yet it made Jacob ponder about the eagerness with which the children attended his church. It seemed to him then that his church was the only place in which they could relax, sing, and play together. He determined to have no more sermons, only singing and play. Perhaps the Lord had seen all the hardships children endured. But he did not mention this to his wife as half his mind approved of the way she brought up the children. Half of the customs too agreed with the many good things the Lord had pointed out to Jacob. From their mother's training, they broke the crust of bread and shared it equally with each other or any other child who happened to be passing by. Jacob pondered on all these things shown him by his new wife, and also the customs which she followed so strictly to teach her children the correct way of living with others.

One other thing caused a stir of amazement in Makaleng village. Jacob now had a family but his occupation brought him no funds. There were two boys of school-going age who needed clothes and school fees. Therefore Jacob spent each morning doing odd jobs about the village to have a small amount of money in hand for whatever his family might need. The women of the village said Johannah was indeed blessed to have such a good man. If Prophet Jacob had condescended to be a priest like Prophet Lebojang, he could have got people to contribute handsomely to his church. But Prophet Jacob always said: 'Please get permission from your Maruti before you join my church.' And which priest would give this permission when it meant losing one of his pay packets?

* * *

Not long after these discussions of the people of Makaleng, the world came crashing down on Prophet Lebojang. It all began simply enough. A certain man of Makaleng village, named Kelepile, was detained on business in the big railway village thirty miles away. He had missed the last transport home and decided to make the journey by foot. As he approached Makaleng he noticed a big car parked on one side of the road and from the bushes nearby he heard voices raised in argument. Being merely curious about what people could be doing in the bushes at night, he turned and crept near. Soon he was able to hear the conversation quite clearly.

An alien voice was saying: 'It's always the case with you, Lebojang. You always want the best parts of the body.'

Lebojang appeared to be very cross. He said, 'I'm telling you, Bogosi, you won't get the money if you don't hand the heart over to me.'

The man, Kelepile, waited to hear no more. In fact, his legs were shaking with terror. He has often said that he cannot recollect how they brought him with such speed into Makaleng village. He knew well enough that the conversation was about a ritual murder, just committed. The first thought in his mind had been to save his own life but to his amazement he found his shaking legs taking him to the police station. And this was how it came about that the police surrounded Lebojang and two other men, one of whom was a witch-doctor by profession and the other a chief. They arrested the three men with the cut up parts of a dead child in their hands. This was the first time that the doers of these evil deeds had been caught in the act. Often the mutilated bodies were found but the murderers were seldom caught.

The position was desperate. The chief and witch-doctor immediately turned state witness and shifted the blame to Lebojang. The witch-doctor was so obliging as to point out to the authorities the graves of twenty other victims to fix the case against Lebojang. They said they did this sort of murder to make potions for the cattle of rich men, like the chief, to increase. Lebojang could even make rain. Lebojang's potions had long been recommended as the best in the land. He had been making these potions and killing men, women, and children for twenty years. He had also been the priest of a Christian church with a big blue cross down the back of his cloak.

Lebojang was sentenced to death. But the story did not end there. A strange thing happened after Lebojang's death. People say the soul of Lebojang returned from the grave. At night, it kept on knocking on the doors of all the people to whom he had sold potions. Some of these people packed their belongings and fled. Some went insane. Some people also say that Lebojang's soul is like that of Lazarus. Lebojang only wanted to tell the people whom he awoke at night—his fellow ritual murderers—to desist from taking the lives of people because of the agony he was suffering now.

Life

In 1963, when the borders were first set up between Botswana and South Africa, pending Botswana's independence in 1966, all Botswana-born citizens had to return home. Everything had been mingled up in the old colonial days, and the traffic of people to and fro between the two countries had been a steady flow for years and years. More often, especially if they were migrant labourers working in the mines, their period of settlement was brief, but many people had settled there in permanent employment. It was these settlers who were disrupted and sent back to village life in a mainly rural country. On their return they brought with them bits and bits of a foreign culture and city habits which they had absorbed. Village people reacted in their own way; what they liked, and was beneficial to them—they absorbed, for instance, the faith-healing cult churches which instantly took hold like wildfire—what was harmful to them, they rejected. The murder of Life had this complicated undertone of rejection.

Life had left the village as a little girl of ten years old with her parents for Johannesburg. They had died in the meanwhile, and on Life's return, seventeen years later, she found, as was village custom, that she still had a home in the village. On mentioning that her name was Life Morapedi, the villagers immediately and obligingly took her to the Morapedi yard in the central part of the village. The family yard had remained intact, just as they had left it, except that it looked pathetic in its desolation. The thatch of the mud huts had patches of soil over them where the ants had made their nests; the wooden poles that supported the rafters of the huts had tilted to an angle as their base had been eaten through by the ants. The rubber hedge had grown to a disproportionate size and enclosed the yard in a gloom of shadows that kept out the sunlight. Weeds and grass of many seasonal rains entangled themselves in the yard.

Life's future neighbours, a group of women, continued to stand near her.

'We can help you to put your yard in order,' they said kindly. 'We are very happy that a child of ours has returned home.'

They were impressed with the smartness of this city girl. They generally wore old clothes and kept their very best things for special occasions like weddings, and even then those best things might just be ordinary cotton prints. The girl wore an expensive cream costume of linen material, tailored to fit her tall, full figure. She had a bright, vivacious friendly manner and laughed freely and loudly. Her speech was rapid and a little hysterical but that was in keeping with her whole personality.

'She is going to bring us a little light,' the women said among themselves, as they went off to fetch their work tools. They were always looking 'for the light' and by that they meant that they were ever alert to receive new ideas that would freshen up the ordinariness and everydayness of village life.

A woman who lived near the Morapedi yard had offered Life hospitality until her own yard was set in order. She picked up the shining new suitcases and preceded Life to her own home, where Life was immediately surrounded with all kinds of endearing attentions—a low stool was placed in a shady place for her to sit on; a little girl came shyly forward with a bowl of water for her to wash her hands; and following on this, a tray with a bowl of meat and porridge was set before her so that she could revive herself after her long journey home. The other women briskly entered her yard with hoes to scratch out the weeds and grass, baskets of earth and buckets of water to re-smear the mud walls, and they had found two idle men to rectify the precarious tilt of the wooden poles of the mud hut. These were the sort of gestures people always offered, but they were pleased to note that the newcomer seemed to have an endless stream of money which she flung around generously. The work party in her yard would suggest that the meat of a goat, slowly simmering in a great iron pot, would help the work to move with a swing, and Life would immediately produce the money to purchase the goat and also tea, milk, sugar, pots of porridge or anything the workers expressed a preference for, so that those two weeks of making Life's yard beautiful for her seemed like one long wedding-feast; people usually only ate that much at weddings.

'How is it you have so much money, our child?' one of the women at last asked, curiously.

'Money flows like water in Johannesburg,' Life replied, with her gay and hysterical laugh. 'You just have to know how to get it.'

The women received this with caution. They said among themselves that their child could not have lived a very good life in Johannesburg. Thrift and honesty were the dominant themes of village life and everyone knew that one could not be honest and rich at the same time; they counted every penny and knew how they had acquired it—with hard work. They never imagined money as a bottomless pit without end; it always had an end and was hard to come by in this dry, semi-desert land. They predicted that she would soon settle down—intelligent girls got jobs in the post office sooner or later.

Life had had the sort of varied career that a city like Johannesburg offered a lot of black women. She had been a singer, beauty queen, advertising model, and prostitute. None of these careers were available in the village—for the illiterate women there was farming and housework; for the literate, teaching, nursing, and clerical work. The first wave of women Life attracted to herself were the farmers and housewives. They were the intensely conservative hard-core centre of village life. It did not take them long to shun her completely because men started turning up in an unending stream. What caused a stir of amazement was that Life was the first and the only woman in the village to make a business out of selling herself. The men were paying her for her services. People's attitude to sex was broad and generous—it was recognised as a necessary part of human life, that it ought to be available whenever possible like food and water, or else one's life would be extinguished or one would get dreadfully ill. To prevent these catastrophes from happening, men and women generally had quite a lot of sex but on a respectable and human level, with financial considerations coming in as an afterthought. When the news spread around that this had now become a business in Life's yard, she attracted to herself a second wave of women—the beer-brewers of the village.

The beer-brewing women were a gay and lovable crowd who had emancipated themselves some time ago. They were drunk every day and could be seen staggering around the village, usually with a wide-eyed, illegitimate baby hitched on to their hips. They also talked and laughed loudly and slapped each other on the back and had developed a language all their own:

'Boyfriends, yes. Husbands, uh, uh, no. Do this! Do that! We want to rule ourselves.'

But they too were subject to the respectable order of village life. Many men passed through their lives but they were all for a time steady boyfriends. The usual arrangement was:

'Mother, you help me and I'll help you.'

This was just so much eye-wash. The men hung around, lived on the resources of the women, and during all this time they would part with about

R2.00 of their own money. After about three months a tally-up would be made:

'Boyfriend,' the woman would say. 'Love is love and money is money. You owe me money.' And he'd never be seen again, but another scoundrel would take his place. And so the story went on and on. They found their queen in Life and like all queens, they set her activities apart from themselves; they never attempted to extract money from the constant stream of men because they did not know how, but they liked her yard. Very soon the din and riot of a Johannesburg township was duplicated, on a minor scale, in the central part of the village. A transistor radio blared the day long. Men and women reeled around drunk and laughing and food and drink flowed like milk and honey. The people of the surrounding village watched this phenomenon with pursed lips and commented darkly:

'They'll all be destroyed one day like Sodom and Gomorrah.'

Life, like the beer-brewing women, had a language of her own too. When her friends expressed surprise at the huge quantities of steak, eggs, liver, kidneys, and rice they ate in her yard—the sort of food they too could now and then afford but would not dream of purchasing—she replied in a carefree, off-hand way: 'I'm used to handling big money.' They did not believe it; they were too solid to trust to this kind of luck which had such shaky foundations, and as though to offset some doom that might be just around the corner they often brought along their own scraggy, village chickens reared in their yards, as offerings for the day's round of meals. And one of Life's philosophies on life, which they were to recall with trembling a few months later, was: 'My motto is: live fast, die young, and have a good-looking corpse.' All this was said with the bold, free joy of a woman who had broken all the social taboos. They never followed her to those dizzy heights.

A few months after Life's arrival in the village, the first hotel with its pub opened. It was initially shunned by all the women and even the beer-brewers considered they hadn't fallen *that* low yet—the pub was also associated with the idea of selling oneself. It became Life's favourite business venue. It simplified the business of making appointments for the following day. None of the men questioned their behaviour, nor how such an un-natural situation had been allowed to develop—they could get all the sex they needed for free in the village, but it seemed to fascinate them that they should pay for it for the first time. They had quickly got to the stage where they communicated with Life in short-hand language:

'When?' And she would reply: 'Ten o'clock.' 'When?' 'Two o'clock.'

'When?' 'Four o'clock,' and so on.

And there would be the roar of cheap small talk and much buttock slapping. It was her element and her feverish, glittering, brilliant black eyes swept around the bar, looking for everything and nothing at the same time.

Then one evening death walked quietly into the bar. It was Lesego, the cattle-man, just come in from his cattle-post, where he had been occupied for a period of three months. Men built up their own, individual reputations in the village and Lesego's was one of the most respected and honoured. People said of him: 'When Lesego has got money and you need it, he will give you what he has got and he won't trouble you about the date of payment . . .' He was honoured for another reason also—for the clarity and quiet indifference of his thinking. People often found difficulty in sorting out issues or the truth in any debatable matter. He had a way of keeping his head above water, listening to an argument and always pronouncing the final judgement: 'Well, the truth about this matter is . . .' He was also one of the most successful cattle-men with a balance of R7.000 in the bank, and whenever he came into the village he lounged around and gossiped or attended village kgotla meetings, so that people had a saying: 'Well, I must be getting about my business. I'm not like Lesego with money in the bank.'

As usual, the brilliant radar eyes swept feverishly around the bar. They did the rounds twice that evening in the same manner, each time coming to a dead stop for a full second on the thin, dark concentrated expression of Lesego's face. There wasn't any other man in the bar with that expression; they all had sheepish, inane-looking faces. He was the nearest thing she had seen for a long time to the Johannesburg gangsters she had associated with— the same small, economical gestures, the same power and control. All the men near him quietened down and began to consult with him in low earnest voices; they were talking about the news of the day which never reached the remote cattle-posts. Whereas all the other men had to approach her, the third time her radar eyes swept round he stood his ground, turned his head slowly, and then jerked it back slightly in a silent command:

'Come here.'

She moved immediately to his end of the bar.

'Hullo,' he said, in an astonishingly tender voice and a smile flickered across his dark, reserved face. That was the sum total of Lesego, that basically he was a kind and tender man, that he liked women and had been so successful in that sphere that he took his dominance and success for granted. But they looked at each other from their own worlds and came to fatal conclusions—she saw in him the power and maleness of the gangsters;

he saw the freshness and surprise of an entirely new kind of woman. He had left all his women after a time because they bored him, and like all people who live an ordinary humdrum life, he was attracted to that under-tone of hysteria in her.

Very soon they stood up and walked out together. A shocked silence fell upon the bar. The men exchanged looks with each other and the way these things communicate themselves, they knew that all the other appointments had been cancelled while Lesego was there. And as though speaking their thoughts aloud, Sianana, one of Lesego's friends commented: 'Lesego just wants to try it out like we all did because it is something new. He won't stay there when he finds out that it is rotten to the core.'

But Sianana was to find out that he did not fully understand his friend. Lesego was not seen at his usual lounging-places for a week and when he emerged again it was to announce that he was to marry. The news was received with cold hostility. Everyone talked of nothing else; it was as impossible as if a crime was being committed before their very eyes. Sianana once more made himself the spokesman. He waylaid Lesego on his way to the village kgotla:

'I am much surprised by the rumours about you, Lesego,' he said bluntly. 'You can't marry that woman. She's a terrible fuck-about!'

Lesego stared back at him steadily, then he said in his quiet, indifferent way: 'Who isn't here?'

Sianana shrugged his shoulders. The subtleties were beyond him; but whatever else was going on it wasn't commercial, it was human, but did that make it any better? Lesego liked to bugger up an argument like that with a straightforward point. As they walked along together Sianana shook his head several times to indicate that something important was eluding him, until at last with a smile, Lesego said: 'She has told me all about her bad ways. They are over.'

Sianana merely compressed his lips and remained silent.

Life made the announcement too, after she was married, to all her beer-brewing friends: 'All my old ways are over,' she said. 'I have now become a woman.'

She still looked happy and hysterical. Everything came to her too easily, men, money, and now marriage. The beer-brewers were not slow to point out to her with the same amazement with which they had exclaimed over the steak and eggs, that there were many women in the village who had cried their eyes out over Lesego. She was very flattered.

Their lives, at least Lesego's, did not change much with marriage. He still liked lounging around the village; the rainy season had come and life was easy for the cattle-men at this time because there was enough water and grazing for the animals. He wasn't the kind of man to fuss about the house and during this time he only made three pronouncements about the household. He took control of all the money. She had to ask him for it and state what it was to be used for. Then he didn't like the transistor radio blaring the whole day long.

'Women who keep that thing going the whole day have nothing in their heads,' he said.

Then he looked down at her from a great height and commented finally and quietly: 'If you go with those men again, I'll kill you.'

This was said so indifferently and quietly, as though he never really expected his authority and dominance to encounter any challenge.

She hadn't the mental equipment to analyse what had hit her, but something seemed to strike her a terrible blow behind the head. She instantly succumbed to the blow and rapidly began to fall apart. On the surface, the everyday round of village life was deadly dull in its even, unbroken monotony; one day slipped easily into another, drawing water, stamping corn, cooking food. But within this there were enormous tugs and pulls between people. Custom demanded that people care about each other, and all day long there was this constant traffic of people in and out of each other's lives. Someone had to be buried; sympathy and help were demanded for this event—there were money loans, new-born babies, sorrow, trouble, gifts. Lesego had long been the king of this world; there was, every day, a long string of people, wanting something or wanting to give him something in gratitude for a past favour. It was the basic strength of village life. It created people whose sympathetic and emotional responses were always fully awakened, and it rewarded them by richly filling in a void that was one big, gaping yawn. When the hysteria and cheap rowdiness were taken away, Life fell into the yawn; she had nothing inside herself to cope with this way of life that had finally caught up with her. The beer-brewing women were still there; they still liked her yard because Lesego was casual and easy-going and all that went on in it now—like the old men squatting in corners with gifts: 'Lesego, I had good luck with my hunting today. I caught two rabbits and I want to share one with you . . .'—was simply the Tswana way of life they too lived. In keeping with their queen's new status, they said:

'We are women and must do something.'

They collected earth and dung and smeared and decorated Life's court-yard. They drew water for her, stamped her corn, and things looked quite ordinary on the surface because Lesego also liked a pot of beer. No one noticed the expression of anguish that had crept into Life's face. The boredom of the daily round was almost throttling her to death and no matter which way she looked, from the beer-brewers to her husband to all the people who called, she found no one with whom she could communicate what had become an actual physical pain. After a month of it, she was near collapse. One morning she mentioned her agony to the beer-brewers: 'I think I have made a mistake. Married life doesn't suit me.'

And they replied sympathetically: 'You are just getting used to it. After all it's a different life in Johannesburg.'

The neighbours went further. They were impressed by a marriage they thought could never succeed. They started saying that one never ought to judge a human being who was both good and bad, and Lesego had turned a bad woman into a good woman which was something they had never seen before. Just as they were saying this and nodding their approval, Sodom and Gomorrah started up all over again. Lesego had received word late in the evening that the new born calves at his cattle-post were dying, and early the next morning he was off again in his truck.

The old, reckless wild woman awakened from a state near death with a huge sigh of relief. The transistor blared, the food flowed again, the men and women reeled around dead drunk. Simply by their din they beat off all the unwanted guests who nodded their heads grimly. When Lesego came back they were going to tell him this was no wife for him.

Three days later Lesego unexpectedly was back in the village. The calves were all anaemic and they had to be brought in to the vet for an injection. He drove his truck straight through the village to the vet's camp. One of the beer-brewers saw him and hurried in alarm to her friend.

'The husband is back,' she whispered fearfully, pulling Life to one side.

'Agh,' she replied irritably.

She did dispel the noise, the men, and the drink, but a wild anger was driving her to break out of a way of life that was like death to her. She told one of the men she'd see him at six o'clock. At about five o'clock Lesego drove into the yard with the calves. There was no one immediately around to greet him. He jumped out of the truck and walked to one of the huts, pushing open the door. Life was sitting on the bed. She looked up silently and sullenly. He was a little surprised but his mind was still distracted by the calves. He had to settle them in the yard for the night.

'Will you make some tea,' he said. 'I'm very thirsty.'

'There's no sugar in the house,' she said. 'I'll have to get some.'

Something irritated him but he hurried back to the calves and his wife walked out of the yard. Lesego had just settled the calves when a neighbour walked in, he was very angry.

'Lesego,' he said bluntly. 'We told you not to marry that woman. If you go to the yard of Radithobolo now you'll find her in bed with him. Go and see for yourself that you may leave that bad woman!'

Lesego stared quietly at him for a moment, then at his own pace as though there were no haste or chaos in his life, he went to the hut they used as a kitchen. A tin full of sugar stood there. He turned and found a knife in the corner, one of the large ones he used for slaughtering cattle, and slipped it into his shirt. Then at his own pace he walked to the yard of Radithobolo. It looked deserted, except that the door of one of the huts was partially open and one closed. He kicked open the door of the closed hut and the man within shouted out in alarm. On seeing Lesego he sprang cowering into a corner. Lesego jerked his head back indicating that the man should leave the room. But Radithobolo did not run far. He wanted to enjoy himself so he pressed himself into the shadows of the rubber hedge. He expected the usual husband-and-wife scene—the irate husband cursing at the top of his voice; the wife, hysterical in her lies and self-defence. Only Lesego walked out of the yard and he held in his hand a huge, blood-stained knife. On seeing the knife Radithobolo immediately fell to the ground in a dead faint. There were a few people on the footpath and they shrank into the rubber hedge at the sight of that knife.

Very soon a wail arose. People clutched at their heads and began running in all directions crying yo! yo! yo! in their shock. It was some time before anyone thought of calling the police. They were so disordered because murder, outright and violent, was a most uncommon and rare occurrence in village life. It seemed that only Lesego kept cool that evening. He was sitting quietly in his yard when the whole police force came tearing in. They looked at him in horror and began to thoroughly upbraid him for looking so unperturbed.

'You have taken a human life and you are cool like that!' they said angrily. 'You are going to hang by the neck for this. It's a serious crime to take a human life.'

He did not hang by the neck. He kept that cool, head-above-water indifferent look, right up to the day of his trial. Then he looked up at the judge and said calmly: 'Well, the truth about this matter is, I had just returned from the cattle-post. I had had trouble with my calves that day. I came home late and being thirsty, asked my wife to make me tea. She said there was no sugar in the house and left to buy some. My neighbour, Mathata came in after this and said that my wife was not at the shops but in the yard of Radithobolo. He said I ought to go and see what she was doing in the yard of Radithobolo. I thought I would check up about the sugar first and in the kitchen I found a tin full of it. I was sorry and surprised to see this. Then a fire seemed to fill my heart. I thought that if she was doing a bad thing with Radithobolo as Mathata said, I'd better kill her because I cannot understand a wife who could be so corrupt . . .'

Lesego had been doing this for years, passing judgement on all aspects of life in his straightforward, uncomplicated way. The judge, who was a white man, and therefore not involved in Tswana custom and its debates, was as much impressed by Lesego's manner as all the village men had been.

'This is a crime of passion,' he said sympathetically. 'So there are extenuating circumstances. But it is still a serious crime to take a human life so I sentence you to five years imprisonment . . .'

Lesego's friend, Sianana, who was to take care of his business affairs while he was in jail, came to visit Lesego still shaking his head. Something was eluding him about the whole business, as though it had been planned from the very beginning.

'Lesego,' he said, with deep sorrow. 'Why did you kill that fuck-about? You had legs to walk away. You could have walked away. Are you trying to show us that rivers never cross here? There are good women and good men but they seldom join their lives together. It's always this mess and foolishness . . .'

A song by Jim Reeves was very popular at that time: *That's What Happens When Two Worlds Collide*. When they were drunk, the beer-brewing women used to sing it and start weeping. Maybe they had the last word on the whole affair.

Witchcraft

It was one of the most potent evils in the society and people afflicted by it often suffered from a kind of death-in-life. Everything in the society was a mixture of centuries of acquired wisdom and experience, so witchcraft belonged there too; something people had carried along with them from ancestral times. Every single villager believes that at some stage in his life 'something' got hold of him; all his animals died and his life was completely smashed up. They could give long and vivid accounts of what happened to them at this time. The accounts were as solid as the reasons people give for believing in God or Jesus Christ, so that one cannot help but conclude that if a whole society creates a belief in something, that something is likely to become real. But unlike Christianity which proposed the belief in a tender and merciful God eager to comfort and care for man, there was nothing pleasant in this 'dark thing' in village life. It was entirely a force of destruction which people experienced at many levels. Since in olden times, the supreme power of sorcery or witchcraft was vested in the chiefs or rulers, it can be assumed that this force had its source in a power structure that needed an absolute control over the people. Over the years it had become dispersed throughout the whole society like a lingering and malignant ailment that was difficult to cure. Political independence seemed to have aggravated the disease more than anything else because people now said: 'Our old people used to say that you can't kill someone who is not your relative. You know what you are going to take from your relative. But these days they are killing everyone from jealousy . . .'

This anxiety, that people were vulnerable to attack or to assault from an evil source, was always present; so that when an ordinary villager started a new yard and before he put up his fence, he would call the Tswana doctor to place protective charms and medicines all around the yard. He would call the Tswana doctor for almost every event in his life: for herbs to protect him in his employment, when he married, when his children were born, or when he was taking a long journey from home. Since supposedly the society was both Christian and rational, people laughingly explained their behaviour thus: 'The baloi are troubling us. The baloi are those people with a bad heart. No one openly walks around with the mark of the baloi, so we don't know who they are. Very often I can be your friend and laugh and joke with you. Then I see that your life is picking up and your goods are increasing, so I go to the Tswana doctor for medicine to kill you just because I am jealous. White people are better. They might suffer from jealousy but they don't know how to kill people in this way. Batswana people know how to kill. This is how they kill: some day, some one might approach me for four teaspoons of tea leaves, which I lend to him because I think he is in need. But he takes these tea leaves straight to a Tswana doctor who makes a medicine out of it. Suddenly, my whole life falls apart; a sickness enters my body and I am ill from one day to the next. Before I can pass away, I go and consult a Tswana doctor. He throws the bones and straightaway sees the cause of my sickness. He says to me: "You remember you gave so-and-so four teaspoons of tea leaves? Well, he is injuring your life." If life is like this, then all the people are afraid of each other. There is a tendency these days for people to dislike consulting the Tswana doctor because they often find that he has not the power to drive out the baloi and they often waste money consulting him. But the baloi are troubling people . . .'

To complicate matters further, people often used their own resources and wisdom to explain ailments like malnutrition and malaria fever or any other kind of ordinary sickness that could be treated in a hospital, so that everything in the end was reduced to witchcraft. And yet, tentatively, one could concede that there was a terrible horror present in the society. Was it only human evil, that in some inexplicable way could so direct its energies that it had the power to inflict intense suffering or even death on others?

Mma-Mabele belonged to that section of the village who rationalised quite clearly: 'I know I can be poisoned and so meet my end, but I cannot be bewitched. I don't believe in it.' They were the offspring of families who had deeply embraced Christianity and who were regular church-goers; when the hospital opened in the village, they had all their ailments attended to there and did not need to consult the Tswana doctor. All this provided some mental leverage to sort out the true from the false in the everyday round of village life, but not immunity to strange forms of assault.

Of all the people in her village ward, Mma-Mabele lived one of the most unspectacular lives. She had been born in a year when people had reaped a particularly rich harvest of corn and she was named, Mma-Mabele, the corn mother, after this event, Also, the contentment and peace people feel when assured of a year's supply of food seemed deeply woven into her personality. She moved around the village quietly, never seeming flustered or anxious about anything. When her parents and grand-parents were alive, she had shared with them the rhythmic life of people who live off what they can reap from the earth; but on their death she seemed to find herself incapable of moving out to the lands for the ploughing season, so that their land lay fallow now with no one to plough it. Her family was reduced to her sister Maggie and her illegitimate son, Banophi, herself and her own illegitimate child, Virginiah. For a year after the death of all the elderly relatives, her sister Maggie had held down a job as a housekeeper; while Mma-Mabele had moved out into the village and offered to do any chores village women might need done for the day, in return for which she might either be given a plate of food or a dish of corn meal for her own house. They managed badly, and on some days only had water to drink.

Over a number of years, after the birth of her child, Mma-Mabele had acquired an unpleasant nickname in her surroundings. She was called 'he-man' and it was meant to imply that something was not quite right with her genitals, they were mixed up, a combination of male and female. The rumour had been spread by a number of men who had made approaches to her and whom she had turned down with quiet finality: 'I don't want to show myself anymore,' she'd said.

The men never looked up as far as a quiet, sensitive face that might have suffered insult or injury. The only value women were given in the society was their ability to have sex; there was nothing beyond that. Mma-Mabele had been engaged to be married to the man by whom she had had her child; at least he had mentioned it before she conceived. Then he said nothing more and as soon as it could be seen that a baby was on the way, he simply disappeared from the village. There was nothing else to learn from men who boasted: 'We pick them off on our fingers, one-two-three-four-five!' There was nothing else to replace the knowledge that a man and a woman belonged together, in a family circle. What the men resented, because it was rare, was to come face to face with a woman not necessarily in a frenzy about satisfying her genitals, as they did. So they spread the nickname, 'he-man' for Mma-Mabele. But her ability to observe that life was all wrong and a deep sensitivity to feel pain and desist from repeating errors, was all that stood between her and the misery that was soon to engulf her life.

Towards the end of the year when they had struggled so much, Mma-

Mabele also found a job as a housekeeper with a particularly good employer who was impressed with her quiet, respectful personality and her ability to work hard in a neat, orderly way. At the end of the month Mma-Mabele came home heaped with treasures, a salary which was twice that of her sister Maggie, a number of old cotton dresses and a pair of shoes. The two sisters made tea, then as darkness fell they sat outdoors, their backs leaning against the mud wall of a hut, and happily pooled their salaries together on Mma-Mabele's lap. Between them they had a fortune, in terms of village economics: R5.00 of Maggie's salary and R10.00 of Mma-Mabele's salary. Mma-Mabele's salary alone could feed the whole family for a month. So she sat with her head to one side, and with a thoughtful, serious face, worked out their budget for the month.

'I think we should start off by buying half a bag of corn,' she said. 'It will last us two months and give us time to pick up a little . . .'

Maggie nodded her consent. Corn or mabele always lasted longer than half a bag of mealie meal because when the corn was stamped it was separated into two heaps; one of rough grains and one of smoother, stamped grains. The heap of rough grains was cooked first for about ten minutes, to which was then added the heap of smoothly-pounded grain. This technique swelled the pot of porridge to an enormous size.

'After I've spent R6.00 on the bag of corn,' Mma-Mabele continued, 'I'd like to buy one bag of bread flour and cooking oil for fat cakes so that we can have a change of food. That leaves us R1.60 for meat for sixteen days and so my money is finished now.'

With a smile she handed the R5.00 back to Maggie.

'I think you would like to spend this money on clothes,' she said. 'Banophi's school shirts are in tatters and a dress for Virginiah only costs sixty cents; there will still be something left over for a dress for yourself if you like. For myself, I have need of nothing now.'

As Maggie put the R5.00 note in her pocket, Mma-Mabele added wistfully: 'If I can keep this job, we'll soon see what we are making of our lives. Perhaps some of the money can be saved.'

They all ate well that night, heaped plates of porridge and tripe, with the greasy intestinal fat of the ox richly spread over the porridge, and deeply contented the whole family went to sleep. But the following morning, the strange story began.

They were all seated outdoors, eating a breakfast of soft porridge when the small boy, Banophi, began to stare intently at Mma-Mabele's head. At last he remarked: 'Why have you cut your hair, my aunt?'

Mma-Mabele paused, surprised in the act of putting a spoonful of porridge into her mouth.

'But I haven't cut my hair, Banophi,' she said.

'But you have cut it, aunt,' he said. 'There's a smooth patch cut out on the side of your head.'

Apprehensively, Mma-Mabele raised her hand to the right side of her head and with suddenly trembling fingers felt the smooth, bald patch. Her fingers recoiled in alarm. But in a quick, practical, decisive way, she stood up and went to examine the nearly bare interior of her hut. The sleeping mats were neatly folded in a corner; a tin trunk with her clothes stood in another corner and she bent over and searched the bare earth floor for traces of her cut hair. There was nothing. No flesh and blood human being could have entered her hut at night; she had herself unlatched the door from the inside in the early morning. For a moment, she leaned one hand against the earth wall of the hut, faint with fear. In village lore, it was only one thing that could have touched her life—the baloi. On an impulse, to rid herself of the hideous, unknown presence that had invaded her life during the night, she walked back to her sister who was still seated near the fire eating her porridge and said: 'Maggie, you must cut off all my hair before I go to work. I cannot walk around like this.'

'What can the matter be?' Maggie asked, frightened.

'I think it is the baloi who have come to me,' Mma-Mabele said, almost in the same matter-of-fact voice with which she had discussed their budget the night before.

'You should go and see the prophet of the church or I can tell Lekena. Lekena knows about these things. They might help us,' Maggie said.

'Both the prophet and Lekena will want money from me,' Mma-Mabele replied aggressively. 'And where am I to get it? We are poor. But I don't believe in them, so we must keep this trouble to ourselves.'

Maggie, as the younger sister, kept silent. Mma-Mabele was the strength of the household and all her judgements on life and people were sane and kind. Obediently Maggie cut off all her hair, then they both left home for work. It was a Saturday morning, and the children, who were not at school that day, spread around the story of the patch of hair that had been cut out on Mma-Mabele's head in a mysterious way during the night. The news soon reached Lekena, the Tswana doctor of their village ward, who lived barely ten yards away from Mma-Mabele.

'I have a customer,' he said to himself.

When Mma-Mabele returned from work late that afternoon, she found

Lekena patiently seated in her yard. He greeted her with unconcealed proprietory interest.

'I say, Mma-Mabele,' he said, astonished. 'You have cut your hair! What have you done with the cut hair?'

'I burnt it,' she said, seating herself politely near him.

'It's a good thing you have destroyed the very thing with which your enemy wishes to injure you. I must say I was very surprised when the story reached me this morning. I thought: "Who could want to injure a kind woman like Mma-Mabele? She has harmed no one. I must rush to help her".' With these words, he reached under his low stool and dramatically produced a bottle of dark medicine.

Mma-Mabele had been looking at him with an appeal-for-help expression on her face. It was the first time in her life that the baloi had visited her and she was deeply afraid of the event. But when he produced the bottle of medicine, she compressed her lips firmly. He would ask for R5.00 and she had no intention of parting with her money.

'I cannot take the medicine, Lekena,' she said, quickly inventing a defence. 'You know very well I am a church-goer and it is forbidden to us to use Tswana medicine.'

'The church doesn't know everything, Mma-Mabele,' he said earnestly. 'The trouble comes from Tswana custom and it is only Tswana medicine that can help you.'

Like all his clan, the Tswana doctors, Lekena had considerable dash and courage. They were like gymnastic performers of a very imaginative kind and for centuries, in their tradition, they had explained the world of phenomena to themselves and the people. They were the most clever men in the society and their hold on the people was very strong. It took a cold and logical mind to analyse all their activities because in spite of repeated failures in their medical treatment of people, they were still consulted avidly. Coldness and logic were Mma-Mabele's special mental gifts. She had stood apart and watched all Lekena's failures, some of which were of a fatal nature. Lekena claimed to remove the poison of a scorpion bite through his medicine which gave power to his person. For years he appeared successful until the small boy, Molefe, of their village ward had been stung by a big, black scorpion and died while under Lekena's treatment. The same thing happened with snakebite which Lekena also claimed to cure. Mma-Mabele sorted it out for herself—there were poisonous snakes and scorpions and non-poisonous ones. Lekena's treatment only succeeded when the snakes and scorpions were non-poisonous. But what to make out of that cut-out patch of her hair?

'It is true I am puzzled, Lekena' she said. 'I have never seen this thing before on myself. My hair was truly cut out like a smooth part of my skin.'

'There are no secrets here, Mma-Mabele. Everyone knows you now have a good job. Someone is jealous of you and wants you to lose that job,' he said.

At this, she compressed her lips again. No one else had experienced that year of near starvation behind her; at times she had stumbled around faint and dizzy with hunger. Whatever else happened, she wasn't going to lose her job.

'I'll throw the bones for you,' Lekena said persuasively. 'The bones will help me to see the one who is injuring your life. Throwing the bones is cheaper than the medicine. It only costs R1.00.'

Mma-Mabele shook her head slowly. To show that he only had good intentions towards her, Lekena touched his hands over his heart.

'Everyone can see my heart,' he said. 'There is no evil thing in it,' and with this assurance, he departed.

From then onwards Mma-Mabele was to find that it was a deep unhappiness to be afflicted by the things that dwelt in the dark side of human life. Formerly, the stories had come to her by hearsay, but their end was all the same—the people so afflicted sat down and began to rot; they would not work or do anything because they believed that the very attempt to prosper in life had brought the affliction on them; they sat like that until they died. Whereas formerly, her life had been a vaguely pleasant round of work, sleep and idle chatter and gossip, it turned from this sunlit world to an inner world of gloomy brooding and pain.

There was something horribly disturbing about the nights. They always began the same way. She would see a small, pointed yellow light, which was followed by indistinct black shapes that bubbled in front of her with the liquid flow of water. Then she seemed caught up in a high wind-storm and was dashed about this way and that. But more persistent was a sensation that she was being strangled by an unseen hand. Then one night, the source of her affliction took on embodied form. It was a misshapen thing walking towards her, with a huge, misshapen face. She lay on her side that night and the thing, it looked like a grotesque man, bent and placed its mouth on her chest and pressed a forefinger and thumb into her forehead. She was quite powerless to protest or move; she just lay there, her heart wildly pounding with fear. It was some time before she regained her senses and realised that she was quite alone in the dark hut. Thinking she had seen the Devil or worse, she arose trembling and kneeling upright in bed she prayed, piteously: 'Oh

Lord Jesu, help me.'

As she said these words, a soft laugh sounded just behind her ear. She groped around in the dark for matches and lit the small oil lamp beside her bed. Except for herself, the hut was quite empty. She sat up for the rest of the night, too afraid to sleep. At one stage she cried out: 'Oh, poor me, what will become of me now!'

The following morning she felt the pain. Just as she was in the midst of her work at mid-morning, a blow struck her on the head. She slowly rocked from end to end with the violence of it and she held on to the household broom for support. She blinked her eyes rapidly in the intensity of her pain. It was some moments she stood like that, completely immobile, and the pain hanging there like a dull, heavy weight in her head as though an unseen ghoul had fastened its mouth there and was slowly sucking out her brains. This happened repeatedly at the same time each morning, until on the third morning her employer found her like that, clinging to the broom in her pain.

'Why, Mma-Mabele, what's wrong with you?' she asked.

'I think I am sick,' Mma-Mabele replied, fearfully. She had to say it, but she did not want to lose her job. But then neither did her employer want to lose her. Good housekeepers were hard to come by, so she made a sympathetic arrangement for Mma-Mabele to take two days off as sick-leave and go to the hospital for a check-up.

Lekena, who now kept a sharp eye on Mma-Mabele's yard, nodded his head in satisfaction as he saw Mma-Mabele come home long before her work hour was up. She walked with her head bent, broody and mournful and she had a small bag of oranges slung over her left shoulder. She had hardly entered her yard before he followed close on her heels and exclaimed: 'How is it you are so early from work, Mma-Mabele! I am much surprised by this!'

'I am sick, Lekena,' she said. 'I have just come from hospital.'

'What is your sickness, Mma-Mabele?'

'I have a terrible pain in my head.' Then she paused and with a note of surprise in her voice said: 'I was examined by the doctor and he said I am quite a healthy person. Then he asked what food I was eating and he said that crushed corn and meat is not enough; that is poor diet. I should try to eat some oranges too. The pain in my head might be caused by poor food.'

Lekena bent his head in deep thought, then he said: 'They don't know everything Mma-Mabele. I told you your trouble comes from Tswana custom and I can help you too.' He looked at her speculatively: 'I think I know who is injuring you. You do not care about Tswana medicine but I took pity on you and threw the bones, for free. I saw that it is Molema who is injuring your life. He has spread such a bad word about you in the village that I am ashamed to repeat it.'

She looked at Lekena with her steady, honest eyes: 'Molema cannot injure me,' she said. 'He only cares about drink and the bed. Most times he has fallen somewhere, dead drunk. He was angry at one time because I refused to show myself to him, that is why he said that bad word about me. My special parts are quite normal but a woman can be too much hurt by these men, which is why I refuse to show them.'

Not to be outdone by Mma-Mabele's reasoning powers, Lekena said: 'I can throw the bones again, Mma-Mabele. I don't mean you to pay me. Your sickness has worked up my mind. In Tswana custom . . .'

Mma-Mabele jerked her head to one side, impatiently:

'I know we have Tswana custom as well as Christian custom, Lekena. But all the people respect Christian custom. There is no one who would laugh when a person mentions the name of the Lord. This thing which I see now laughs when I pray to the Lord.'

This so knocked Lekena off his medical feet that he drew in his breath with a gasp of surprise: 'You mean you have seen a new thing, Mma-Mabele? I must say I didn't know it. We can never tell what will happen these days, now that we have independence.'

After he had left, she sat in the shadow of the hut and slowly ate some of the oranges, but they didn't help her. She lived with the affliction. Once she realised this, she never asked for sick-leave again. The pain took precedence over everything else she experienced: sometimes it was like a blow in the head; sometimes it was like a blow in the heart—it moved from place to place. Soon her whole village ward noticed the struggle she was waging with death. She became thinner and thinner. She took to leaving very early for work, would walk a little way and then sit down in the pathway to rest. And she did the same on returning home in the evening.

Towards the end of that year her employer and family went away on a month's holiday. The strain to keep her job had reduced Mma-Mabele to a thin skeleton. She seemed about to die. She lay down in her hut like one stunned and dead for many days. Just when everyone expected news of her death, she suddenly recovered and began to eat voraciously and recover her health. She was soon seen about the village at the daily task of drawing water and her friends would stop her and query: 'How is it you aren't sick any more, Mma-Mabele? Did you find a special Tswana doctor to help you, like the rich people?'

And she would reply angrily: 'You all make me sick! There is no one to help the people, not even God. I could not sit down because I am too poor and there is no one else to feed my children.'

Looking for a Rain God

It is lonely at the lands where the people go to plough. These lands are vast clearings in the bush, and the wild bush is lonely too. Nearly all the lands are within walking distance from the village. In some parts of the bush where the underground water is very near the surface, people made little rest camps for themselves and dug shallow wells to quench their thirst while on their journey to their own lands. They experienced all kinds of things once they left the village. They could rest at shady watering places full of lush, tangled trees with delicate pale-gold and purple wild flowers springing up between soft green moss and the children could hunt around for wild figs and any berries that might be in season. But from 1958, a seven-year drought fell upon the land and even the watering places began to look as dismal as the dry open thorn-bush country; the leaves of the trees curled up and withered; the moss became dry and hard and, under the shade of the tangled trees, the ground turned a powdery black and white, because there was no rain. People said rather humorously that if you tried to catch the rain in a cup it would only fill a teaspoon. Towards the beginning of the seventh year of drought, the summer had become an anguish to live through. The air was so dry and moisture-free that it burned the skin. No one knew what to do to escape the heat and tragedy was in the air. At the beginning of that summer, a number of men just went out of their homes and hung themselves to death from trees. The majority of the people had lived off crops, but for two years past they had all returned from the lands with only their rolled-up skin blankets and cooking utensils. Only the charlatans, incanters, and witch-doctors made a pile of money during this time because people were always turning to them in desperation for little talismans and herbs to rub on the plough for the crops to grow and the rain to fall.

The rains were late that year. They came in early November, with a promise of good rain. It wasn't the full, steady downpour of the years of good rain, but thin, scanty, misty rain. It softened the earth and a rich growth of green things sprang up everywhere for the animals to eat. People were called to the village kgotla to hear the proclamation of the beginning of the ploughing season; they stirred themselves and whole families began to move off to the lands to plough.

The family of the old man, Mokgobja, were among those who left early for the lands. They had a donkey cart and piled everything onto it, Mokgobja—who was over seventy years old; two little girls, Neo and Boseyong; their mother Tiro and an unmarried sister, Nesta; and the father and supporter of the family, Ramadi, who drove the donkey cart. In the rush of the first hope of rain, the man, Ramadi, and the two women, cleared the land of thorn-bush and then hedged their vast ploughing area with this same thorn-bush to protect the future crop from the goats they had brought along for milk. They cleared out and deepened the old well with its pool of muddy water and still in this light, misty rain, Ramadi inspanned two oxen and turned the earth over with a hand plough.

The land was ready and ploughed, waiting for the crops. At night, the earth was alive with insects singing and rustling about in search of food. But suddenly, by mid-November, the rain fled away; the rain-clouds fled away and left the sky bare. The sun danced dizzily in the sky, with a strange cruelty. Each day the land was covered in a haze of mist as the sun sucked up the last drop of moisture out of the earth. The family sat down in despair, waiting and waiting. Their hopes had run so high; the goats had started producing milk, which they had eagerly poured on their porridge, now they ate plain porridge with no milk. It was impossible to plant the corn, maize, pumpkin and water-melon seeds in the dry earth. They sat the whole day in the shadow of the huts and even stopped thinking, for the rain had fled away. Only the children, Neo and Boseyong, were quite happy in their little girl world. They carried on with their game of making house like their mother and chattered to each other in light, soft tones. They made children from sticks around which they tied rags, and scolded them severely in an exact imitation of their own mother. Their voices could be heard scolding the day long: 'You stupid thing, when I send you to draw water, why do you spill half of it out of the bucket!' 'You stupid thing! Can't you mind the porridge-pot without letting the porridge burn!' And then they would beat the rag-dolls on their bottoms with severe expressions.

The adults paid no attention to this; they did not even hear the funny chatter; they sat waiting for rain; their nerves were stretched to breaking-point willing the rain to fall out of the sky. Nothing was important, beyond that. All their animals had been sold during the bad years to purchase food, and of all their herd only two goats were left. It was the women of the family who finally broke down under the strain of waiting for rain. It was really the two women who caused the death of the little girls. Each night they started a weird, high-pitched wailing that began on a low, mournful note and whipped up to a frenzy. Then they would stamp their feet and shout as though they had lost their heads. The men sat quiet and self-controlled; it was important for men to maintain their self-control at all times but their nerve was breaking too. They knew the women were haunted by the starvation of the coming year.

Finally, an ancient memory stirred in the old man, Mokgobja. When he was very young and the customs of the ancestors still ruled the land, he had been witness to a rain-making ceremony. And he came alive a little, struggling to recall the details which had been buried by years and years of prayer in a Christian church. As soon as the mists cleared a little, he began consulting in whispers with his youngest son, Ramadi. There was, he said, a certain rain god who accepted only the sacrifice of the bodies of children. Then the rain would fall; then the crops would grow, he said. He explained the ritual and as he talked, his memory became a conviction and he began to talk with unshakable authority. Ramadi's nerves were smashed by the nightly wailing of the women and soon the two men began whispering with the two women. The children continued their game: 'You stupid thing! How could you have lost the money on the way to the shop! You must have been playing again!'

After it was all over and the bodies of the two little girls had been spread across the land, the rain did not fall. Instead, there was a deathly silence at night and the devouring heat of the sun by day. A terror, extreme and deep, overwhelmed the whole family. They packed, rolling up their skin blankets and pots, and fled back to the village.

People in the village soon noted the absence of the two little girls. They had died at the lands and were buried there, the family said. But people noted their ashen, terror-stricken faces and a murmur arose. What had killed the children, they wanted to know? And the family replied that they had just died. And people said amongst themselves that it was strange that the two deaths had occurred at the same time. And there was a feeling of great unease at the unnatural looks of the family. Soon the police came around. The family told them the same story of death and burial at the lands. They did not know what the children had died of. So the police asked to see the graves. At this, the mother of the children broke down and told everything.

Throughout that terrible summer the story of the children hung like a dark cloud of sorrow over the village, and the sorrow was not assuaged when the old man and Ramadi were sentenced to death for ritual murder. All they had on the statute books was that ritual murder was against the law and must be stamped out with the death penalty. The subtle story of strain and starvation and breakdown was inadmissable evidence at court; but all the people who lived off crops knew in their hearts that only a hair's breadth had saved them from sharing a fate similar to that of the Mokgobja family. They could have killed something to make the rain fall.

Kgotla

No day passed without its news, and in the early morning the old men shuffled their way towards the central kgotla of the village, their walking-sticks lightly tapping the ground. Two regular kgotla-goers, Kelapile and Thatayarona, met each other just as they were about to enter the wide, semi-circular wooden enclosure of the kgotla. They each clasped a low, wooden kgotla stool in each left hand and were dressed in their heavy greatcoats as there was a chill in the air. Kelapile was already stooped with age and somewhat absent-minded. Thatayarona was thin, upright, still with a spring in his walk and a loud, authoritative voice that sounded like a deep drum in his chest. They often dominated kgotla affairs together: Kelapile, for his wily insight into human nature; Thatayarona, because he liked to make his voice heard. After they had greeted each other, Kelapile asked:

'What could be the matter under discussion today, Thatayarona? I did not attend afternoon kgotla yesterday as I felt ill, so I do not know the proceedings for today.'

'We heard there was going to be a government pronouncement about a new way of gathering tax,' Thatayarona boomed. 'But I doubt it can be done today because all the headmen have not yet been informed that they should attend kgotla. This news suddenly arrived late in the afternoon, so the pronouncement may be given a day or two later . . .'

They set their stools down near the wooden palings and for a time the two men sat, lost in their own thoughts. Things started leisurely at the kgotla because the chief in charge of it was now old and very ill and given to turning up on duty at any old time.

Behind the kgotla, an administrative block had been set up to modernize village life. It fussed about schools, boreholes, roads, development, and progress; energetic young clerks dashed from one department to another, their hands filled with bureaucratic paperwork. They had no time to listen to the twitter of birds in the ancient shady trees that surrounded the kgotla, but the two worlds daily travelled side by side and the bureaucratic world was fast devouring up the activities of the ancient, rambling kgotla world. They had taken over, from the chief, the duty of land allocation, water rights and things like that, but they hadn't yet taken over people's affairs—the kgotla was still the people's place. It was the last stronghold where people could make their anguish and disputes heard, where nothing new could be said about human nature—it had all been said since time immemorial and it was all of the same pattern, repeating itself from generation unto generation. There, at the kgotla, it wasn't so important to resolve human problems as to discuss around them, to pontificate, to generalize, to display wit, wisdom, wealth of experience or depth of thought. All this made the kgotla world a holy world that moved at its own pace and time and two old men sat dreaming by themselves that early morning.

They stirred a little as a group of people slowly approached the kgotla. As they came near, the two old men noted that the slow movement of the group was due to the fact that they had a blind man in their midst. He was very tall and walked with his hands stiffly at his sides, independent of aid from his companions, but he walked awkwardly with loud, heavy-paced footsteps, lifting his feet too high off the ground each time. He stared ahead of him with wide-open, astonished brown eyes that saw nothing, and every now and then he broke into an angelic, white-toothed smile. The blind man's companions were all women and they sorted themselves out into various groups as they sat down on the ground. A young and good-looking woman, together with an old woman who had her head heavily bandaged, sat on the right side of the blind man; and a group of four women huddled together on his left side. The two old men looked at this strange gathering of people with interest and could make nothing of what their problem could be, but it looked like being an interesting day. Kelapile bent over and whispered to Thatayarona:

'Women are always poking at each other but I wonder who could have tried to kill the old mother?'

Thatayarona chuckled with delight. He already imagined his voice booming over the assembly with witty observations. Just then the old chief arrived in his van and made straight for the kgotla. A number of old men like Kelapile and Thatayarona, who acted as his assessors, also appeared and settled themselves on stools near him. The chief, who these days normally prepared himself to doze when proceedings bored him, also looked at the gathering with interest.

'I believe this case comes from Goo-ra-mere ward,' he began briskly. 'I have received a report about it from headman Serekete who says it has so many complications, he just does not know where to begin.' He paused and asked: 'Who is the owner of this case?'

'I am,' the good-looking young woman said quietly.

'Speak then, let us here what you have to say.'

'It was four years ago that my husband here, Gobosamang, came to Bulawayo to attend at the school for the blind. I was a helper at the school. I liked all his ways at that time, so when he proposed marriage to me, I accepted him. During the year we lived together in my country we were happy and the marriage prospered. It was my husband's idea that we return to his country, but since then nothing has gone right with the marriage. It's the first time I have seen jealousy and spite such as exists in this village and people here have no love or respect for a foreign person. My name is Rose but I hear myself referred to as "that Sindebele woman". It was not long after we arrived that I began to see that people had poisoned my husband against me. Their words to him were that I was taking lovers behind his back and not a day passed when he was not quarrelling with me about this matter. What does it help to say: "The words of those people are not the truth." He cannot see and is dependent on all the poison which is poured into his ears by others. For three years I have lived in misery and the day came when I could stand this strife no more. I thought: "People's jealousy for me is burning my back like a live coal resting there. I shall go back to my own people." I returned to my people but this did not please them because when we married, as is our custom, Gobosamang had offered my people cattle. They feared they would have to return the gifts so they were not pleased by my reappearance. "Oh no," they said, "return to the husband. Jealousy like that is a natural thing. After all, you are a beautiful woman." But I rested there for three months to settle my mind. On my return I found that another woman now occupied my yard and my husband. She had been recently bereaved of her own husband and had made haste to take another. She claims that she offered Gobosamang all her money and worldly goods, which he has already eaten, and she demands that the money and goods be returned. For some days she would not remove herself from the yard and it was only when she had assaulted Gobosamang's mother that he removed her by force.'

Appreciative nods from the chief and his assessors greeted this simple and straightforward statement from the woman Rose, but it was essential to bring out all the points of the case before any comment could be made.

'We have heard you, Rose,' the chief said, already deeply involved in the affair. He shifted his attention to the old woman with the heavily bandaged head: 'Now tell us mother what you have to say.'

'I am Galeboe Lentswe, the mother of Gobosamang here,' she began. 'My son has brought all this trouble on himself, with full awareness, so I have little sympathy for him. He left home for some time and returned with a good and beautiful wife, which was something people did not expect, as he is blind. The marriage filled everyone with wonder and people ever commented that Gobosamang was a lucky man indeed. Then I noticed that this very good luck had created a madness in my son's mind. He could not rest if the wife was not nearby: "Mother, is it not true that my wife has fallen in love with another man? That is what people tell me." He was very nervous about it and I used to pacify him: "No Gobosamang, she has just gone to draw water like any other wife. Besides no one is the owner of any other person, so you should not expect the wife to be tied to you, day and night." But nothing I could say would remove this madness from his head. By the time the wife ran away, I was exhausted. Gobosamang became very ill for a few days. The day I informed him that the wife had run away, he dropped to the ground in a dead faint. I thought he was finished and done for, but no, he stood up after two days and without one word to me, he walked out of the yard and returned a day later with that moswagadi* woman here, Tsietso. I was very shocked and afraid. I approached my son secretly and said: "Gobosamang, you cannot bring a moswagadi into the yard. You know that it is barely three months since her husband passed away and by custom you should not be having relations with a woman like that. You can die." It was as if my son were mad. He would not hear anything I had to say, so I kept quiet and left this unhealthy matter to pursue its course. After three months the wife returned. She said she had been forced by her people to return to her lawful husband and indeed she had her rightful place there as Gobosamang's wife. But do you think we could persuade that moswagadi to leave? She was put up to her rudeness by my son who chose to deliberately ignore his wife. Gobosamang's rightful wife and I were forced to share a hut while he continued to live with the moswagadi. Then, the other day, Gobosamang's wife wanted to make some fat cakes for the evening meal. She prepared the flour and everything, then noticed that there was no cooking fat in the house, so she went to the shop to buy some. On her return she found that the basin of flour had been thrown into a bucket of water: "Who has done this?" she asked. The moswagadi

*moswagadi: a woman recently bereaved of her husband.

was there, looking at her like a snake. She laughed and said: "I'm sure I don't know." But I had seen it all, so I said: "Tsietso, you might have thought I was dozing here but I saw you throw the flour into the water-bucket. And I would advise you to watch your manners and not have too much to say for yourself in our yard. You are the person who is in trouble, not Rose." These were peaceful words, but to my surprise, Tsietso picked up a big stone and threw it at my head. It just missed. Not satisfied with that, she then grabbed me by the ears and pulled them hard. I have a pain in my head to this day. That was when Gobosamang agreed to remove that moswagadi from the yard.'

Trouble and damnation were piling up on the head of the blind man, Gobosamang, so attention next shifted to him.

'Gobosamang,' the chief said, with a surprised expression. 'Tell us if all these things that have so far been said about you are the truth.'

The blind man seemed to be thoroughly enjoying his predicament. That angelic white-toothed smile lit up his face.

'I have nothing to say for myself,' he said. 'I can see that I am in big trouble. But the truth has been spoken so far.'

The chief shook his head slowly expressing his amazement that a blind and handicapped man like Gobosamang could make such an impossible muddle of life. He next turned his attention to the group of four women huddled together.

'I suppose you are the people of Morule ward from which Tsietso comes,' he said. 'Headman Serekete told me that is the ward of Tsietso.'

'Yes, we are the people of Morule ward,' one of the women spoke up. 'And we have accompanied our child Tsietso here to see that justice is done by her at this court. She has given Gobosamang all her money and worldly goods under the false impression that they would start life together. We were surprised to find her cast back into her own yard penniless, and we want all the things she gave to Gobosamang returned.'

'I hear, people of Morule ward,' the chief said. 'Tsietso, tell us your side of the story.'

Tsietso, a tall, thin woman with a loud and vigorous voice looked at the ground with an offended air as she began to speak:

'I was minding my own business, mind you, when Gobosamang came weeping into my yard. "Tsietso," he said. "You are the only one who can understand my pain as you have only recently lost someone you love. My wife is gone and dead by now. I shall never see her again. Let us join our lives together and comfort each other." So I said: "Gobosamang, you know a year of mourning must pass before I can be cleansed and take another man. I am not available." And he said: "Oh, many people have broken custom and no harm has come to them. We don't believe such things any more." I know that as a fact too, that people have broken the custom of observing moswagadi and lived. The trouble with Gobosamang is that he appeals to the heart. He is like a small child who must be cared for and when I saw him weeping like that, my heart was filled with pity and I agreed to his proposal and went to live with him.'

'What are these goods you have given to Gobosamang?' the chief asked.

'I had R300.00 which I gave to Gobosamang,' she said. 'We were to use it for our life together. I gave Gobosamang the money on the understanding that his wife had departed forever. He said we should buy cattle and improve the yard. We were planning all these things together when the wife returned.'

'Gobosamang,' the chief asked. 'Do you still have this R300.00?'

The terrible blind man still smiled: 'We have eaten all of it,' he said. 'Tsietso forgets that she has four children and how were we to feed them every day? I have no employment.'

The essentials of the case having been heard, the court relaxed from its position of attentive listening. It was now time for the assessors and the chief to make known their views on the case. Almost immediately Thata-yarona's drum-like voice rolled over the assembly.

'This case has many profound points,' he said, importantly. 'Let us get back to the point made by Gobosamang's wife, Rose, about jealousy. It would appear as if the good lady has misunderstood our customs. There is no hatred for foreigners. Indeed, the contrary. It is well known from times past that a woman from a far off place has more attraction than the woman who is known and at hand every day. We can see the course of events here. The men found virtue in the foreigner and they were ever commenting about it. This drove the women wild. They said: "Well now, what has Gobosamang's wife got that we haven't got?" So they decided to poison this happy marriage because they were wild with jealousy. It was wrong of Gobosamang to listen to this poison but then he appears a senseless man. That is my point.'

Not to be outdone in making good points, Kelapile followed fast on the heels of his friend with his own observations:

'We see another side of the old story today,' he said, with his profound air of wisdom. 'The forefathers said: "Jealousy starts from the eye." Today we have seen that it is equally troublesome to have no eyes with which to see.

Gobosamang cannot see all the lovers his wife is said to possess and yet he is maddened by jealousy of them. A man with sense would merely observe on being told all these stories: "Well, I am blind. I don't see my wife's lovers, so why should they bother me?" But he is bothered. There is no peace anywhere, either for those who have eyes and for those who have not.'

After this profound statement on life itself, one of the more self-effacing of the assessors said meekly: 'We should not forget that an assault was made on the old mother here and Tsietso ought to explain herself as this is a serious offence.'

At this Tsietso burst into tears briefly.

'Gobosamang's mother would like herself to be known as a saint,' she said. 'But she has a venomous tongue. There was only misery there all the time I lived with Gobosamang. She treated me with scorn. I could not touch any of the household things and had to bring all my own utensils into the yard. A person who is hated is insulted every day, and so a fire built up in my heart against her. By the time I grabbed her by the ears, I no longer knew what I was doing as there was only hatred between us . . .'

It was now time for the chief to pass judgement on the case. He bent his head and spoke as though he had considered all aspects of the matter at hand very carefully.

'Tsietso,' he said. 'The court well understands the complications of this case, but you have caused the old mother pain. She has felt a pain from your assault on her life and for that I fine you R20.00. Now you, Gobosamang, I order you to return the R300.00 you have taken from Tsietso. Also, from now on you are to live in peace with your own true wife. The grievances have been aired and understood, so we consider the matter settled now.'

The crazy blind man looked a little troubled at last.

'I have no way in which I can repay Tsietso the money I am ordered to pay,' he said earnestly. 'I have nothing.'

There was a brief silence. Everyone knew that that was ultimately the crux of the case and it might never be resolved. Then, in the silence, Rose, the wife of Gobosamang spoke very quietly:

'I can get a job in an office somewhere because I know how to do bookkeeping. If Tsietso does not mind, we can then pay back the money owing to her, bit by bit.'

The whole assembly murmured its approval of this noble gesture and the court began to disperse as it was already near the lunch-hour. Thatayarona and Kelapile shuffled away together. As they walked along Kelapile nodded his head profoundly several times.

'I have seen a wonder today, Thatayarona,' he observed at last. 'The Sindebele woman fills me with wonder. You know very well that we can never settle cases at kgotla and this case looked impossible from the start. The forefathers were right when they said that the finest things often come from far-off places . . .'

The Wind and a Boy

Like all the village boys, Friedman had a long wind blowing for him, but perhaps the enchanted wind that blew for him, filled the whole world with magic.

Until they became ordinary, dull grown.men, who drank beer and made babies, the little village boys were a special set all on their own. They were kings whom no one ruled. They wandered where they willed from dawn to dusk and only condescended to come home at dusk because they were afraid of the horrible things in the dark that might pounce on them. Unlike the little girls who adored household chores and drawing water, it was only now and then that the boys showed themselves as useful attachments to any household. When the first hard rains of summer fell, small dark shapes, quite naked except for their loin-cloths, sped out of the village into the bush. They knew that the first downpour had drowned all the wild rabbits, moles, and porcupines in their burrows in the earth. As they crouched down near the entrances to the burrows, they would see a small drowned nose of an animal peeping out; they knew it had struggled to emerge from its burrow, flooded by the sudden rush of storm water and as they pulled out the animal, they would say, pityingly:

'Birds have more sense than rabbits, moles and porcupines. They build their homes in trees.' But it was hunting made easy, for no matter how hard a boy and his dog ran, a wild rabbit ran ten times faster; a porcupine hurled his poisonous quills into the body; and a mole stayed where he thought it was safe—deep under the ground. So it was with inordinate pride that the boys carried home armfuls of dead animals for their families to feast on for many days. Apart from that, the boys lived very much as they pleased, with the wind and their own games.

Now and then, the activities of a single family could captivate the imagination and hearts of all the people of their surroundings; for years and years, the combination of the boy, Friedman and his grandmother,

Sejosenye, made the people of Ga-Sefete-Molemo ward, smile, laugh, then cry.

They smiled at his first two phases. Friedman came home as a small bundle from the hospital, a bundle his grandmother nursed carefully near her bosom and crooned to day and night with extravagant care and tenderness.

'She is like that,' people remarked, 'because he may be the last child she will ever nurse. Sejosenye is old now and will die one of these days; the child is a gift to keep her heart warm.'

Indeed, all Sejosenye's children were grown, married, and had left home. Of all her children, only her last-born daughter was unmarried and Friedman was the result of some casual mating she had indulged in, in a town a hundred miles away where she had a job as a typist. She wanted to return to her job almost immediately, so she handed the child over to her mother and that was that; she could afford to forget him as he had a real mother now. During all the time that Sejosenye haunted the hospital, awaiting her bundle, a friendly foreign doctor named Friedman took a fancy to her maternal, grandmotherly ways. He made a habit of walking out of his path to talk to her. She never forgot it and on receiving her bundle she called the baby, Friedman.

They smiled at his second phase, a small dark shadow who toddled silently and gravely beside a very tall grandmother; wherever the grandmother went, there went Friedman. Most women found this phase of the restless, troublesome toddler tedious; they dumped the toddler onto one of their younger girls and were off to weddings and visits on their own.

'Why can't you leave your handbag at home some times, granny?' they said.

'Oh, he's no trouble,' Sejosenye would reply.

They began to laugh at his third phase. Almost overnight he turned into a tall, spindly-legged, graceful gazelle with large, grave eyes. There was an odd, musical lilt to his speech and when he teased, or was up to mischief, he moved his head on his long thin neck from side to side like a cobra. It was he who became the king of kings of all the boys in his area; he could turn his hand to anything and made the best wire cars with their wheels of shoe polish tins. All his movements were neat, compact, decisive, and for his age he was a boy who knew his own mind. They laughed at his knowingness and certainty on all things, for he was like the grandmother who had had a flaming youth all her own too. Sejosenye had scandalized the whole village in her days of good morals by leaving her own village ward to live with a married man in Ga-Sefete-Molemo ward. She had won him from his wife and married him and then lived down the scandal in the way only natural queens can. Even in old age, she was still impressive. She sailed through the village, head in the air, with a quiet, almost expressionless face. She had developed large buttocks as time went by and they announced their presence firmly in rhythm with her walk.

Another of Sejosenye's certainties was that she was a woman who could plough, but it was like a special gift. Each season, in drought or hail or sun, she removed herself to her lands. She not only ploughed but nursed and brooded over her crops. She was there all the time till the corn ripened and the birds had to be chased off the land, till harvesting and threshing were done; so that even in drought years with their scanty rain, she came home with some crops. She was the envy of all the women of the surroundings.

'Sejosenye always eats fine things in her house,' they said. 'She ploughs and then sits down for many months and enjoys the fruits of her labour.'

The women also envied her beautiful grandson. There was something special there, so that even when Friedman moved into his bad phase, they forgave him crimes other boys received a sound thrashing for. The small boys were terrible thieves who harassed people by stealing their food and money. It was all a part of the games they played but one which people did not like. Of them all, Friedman was the worst thief, so that his name was mentioned more and more in any thieving that had been uncovered.

'But Friedman showed us how to open the window with a knife and string,' the sobbing, lashed boys would protest.

'Friedman isn't as bad as you,' the parents would reply, irrationally. They were hypnotised by a beautiful creature. The boy Friedman, who had become a real nuisance by then, also walked around as though he were special. He couldn't possibly be a thief and he added an aloof, offended, disdainful expression to his pretty face. He wasn't just an ordinary sort of boy in Ga-Sefete-Molemo ward. He was . . .

It happened, quite accidentally, that his grandmother told him all those stories about the hunters, warriors, and emissaries of old. She was normally a quiet, absent-minded woman, given to dreaming by herself but she liked to sing the boy a little song now and then as they sat by the outdoor fire. A lot of them were church songs and rather sad; they more or less passed as her bed-time prayer at night—she was one of the old church-goers. Now and then she added a quaint little song to her repertoire and as the night-time, fire-light flames flickered between them, she never failed to note that this particular song was always well received by the boy. A little light would awaken in his eyes and he would bend forward and listen attentively.

'Welcome, Robinson Crusoe, welcome,' she would sing, in clear, sweet tones. 'How could you stay, so long away, Robinson how could you do so?'

When she was very young, Sejosenye had attended the mission school of the village for about a year; made a slight acquaintance with the ABC and one, two, three, four, five, and the little song about Robinson Crusoe. But girls didn't need an education in those days when ploughing and marriage made up their whole world. Yet Robinson Crusoe lived on as a gay and out-of-context memory of her school-days. One evening the boy leaned forward and asked:

'Is that a special praise-poem song for Robinson Crusoe, grandmother?'

'Oh yes,' she replied, smiling.

'It appears that the people liked Robinson Crusoe much,' the boy observed. 'Did he do great things for them?'

'Oh yes,' she said, smiling.

'What great things did he do?' the boy asked, pointedly.

'They say he was a hunter who went by Gweta side and killed an elephant all by himself,' she said, making up a story on the spot. 'Oh! In those days, no man could kill an elephant by himself. All the regiments had to join together and each man had to thrust his sword into the side of the elephant before it died. Well, Robinson Crusoe was gone many days and people wondered about him: "Perhaps he has been eaten by a lion," they said. "Robinson likes to be a solitary person and do foolish things. We won't ever go out into the bush by ourselves because we know it is dangerous." Well, one day, Robinson suddenly appeared in their midst and people could see that he had a great thing on his mind. They all gathered around him. He said: "I have killed an elephant for all the people." The people were surprised: "Robinson!" they said. "It is impossible! How did you do it? The very thought of an elephant approaching the village makes us shiver!" And Robinson said: "Ah, people, I saw a terrible sight! I was standing at the feet of the elephant. I was just a small ant. I could not see the world any more. Elephant was above me until his very head touched the sky and his ears spread out like great wings. He was angry but I only looked into one eye which was turning round and round in anger. What to do now? I thought it better to put that eye out. I raised my spear and threw it at the angry eye. People! It went right inside. Elephant said not a word and he fell to one side. Come I will show you what I have done." Then the women cried in joy: "Loo-loo-loo!" They ran to fetch their containers as some wanted the meat of the elephant; some wanted the fat. The men made their knives sharp. They would make shoes and many things from the skin and bones. There was something for all the people in the great work Robinson Crusoe did.'

All this while, as he listened to the story, the boy's eyes had glowed softly. At the end of it, he drew in a long breath.

'Grandmother,' he whispered, adroitly stepping into the role of Robinson Crusoe, the great hunter. 'One day, I'm going to be like that. I'm going to be a hunter like Robinson Crusoe and bring meat to all the people.' He paused for breath and then added tensely: 'And what other great thing did Robinson Crusoe do?'

'Tsaa!' she said, clicking her tongue in exhaustion. 'Am I then going away that I must tell *all* the stories at once?'

Although his image of Robinson Crusoe, the great hunter, was never to grow beyond his everyday boyish activities of pushing wire cars, hunting in the fields for wild rabbits, climbing trees to pull down old bird's nests and yelling out in alarm to find that a small snake now occupied the abandoned abode, or racing against the wind with the spoils of his latest theft, the stories awakened a great tenderness in him. If Robinson Crusoe was not churning up the dust in deadly hand-to-hand combat with an enemy, he was crossing swollen rivers and wild jungles as the great messenger and ambassador of the chief—all his activities were touchingly in aid of or in defence of, the people. One day Friedman expressed this awakened compassion for life in a strange way. After a particularly violent storm, people found their huts invaded by many small mice and they were hard-pressed to rid themselves of these pests. Sejosenye ordered Friedman to kill the mice.

'But grandmother,' he protested. 'They have come to us for shelter. They lost all their homes in the storm. It's better that I put them in a box and carry them out into the fields again once the rains are over.'

She had laughed in surprise at this and spread the story around among her women friends, who smiled tenderly then said to their own offspring: 'Friedman isn't as bad as you.'

Life and its responsibilities began to weigh down heavily on Friedman as he approached his fourteenth year. Less time was spent in boyish activities. He grew more and more devoted to his grandmother and concerned to assist her in every way. He wanted a bicycle so that he might run up and down to the shops for her, deliver messages, or do any other chore she might have in mind. His mother, who worked in a town far away, sent him the money to purchase the bicycle. The gift brought the story of his life abruptly to a close.

Towards the beginning of the rainy season, he accompanied his grand-mother to her lands which were some twenty miles outside the village. They sowed seed together after the hired tractor had turned up the land but the boy's main chore was to keep the household pot filled with meat. Sometimes they ate birds Friedman had trapped, sometimes they ate fried tortoise-meat or wild rabbit; but there was always something as the bush abounded with animal life. Sejosenye only had to take a bag of mealie meal, packets of sugar, tea, and powdered milk as provisions for their stay at the lands; meat was never a problem. Mid-way through the ploughing season, she began to run out of sugar, tea, and milk.

'Friedman,' she said that evening. 'I shall wake you early tomorrow morning. You will have to take the bicycle into the village and purchase some more sugar, tea, and milk.'

He was up at dawn with the birds, a solitary figure cycling on a pathway through the empty bush. By nine, he had reached the village and first made his way to Ga-Sefete-Molemo ward and the yard of a friend of his grand-mother, who gave him a cup of tea and a plate of porridge. Then he put one foot on the bicycle and turned to smile at the woman with his beautiful gazelle eyes. His smile was to linger vividly before her for many days as a short while later, hard pounding feet came running into her yard to report that Friedman was dead.

He pushed the bicycle through the winding, sandy pathway of the village ward, reached the high embankment of the main road, peddled vigorously up it and out of the corner of his eye, saw a small green truck speeding towards him. In the devil-may-care fashion of all the small boys, he cycled right into its path, turned his head and smiled appealingly at the driver. The truck caught him on the front bumper, squashed the bicycle and dragged the boy along at a crazy speed for another hundred yards, dropped him and careered on another twenty yards before coming to a halt. The boy's pretty face was a smear all along the road and he only had a torso left.

People of Ga-Sefete-Molemo ward never forgot the last coherent words Sejosenye spoke to the police. A number of them climbed into the police truck and accompanied it to her lands. They saw her walk slowly and enquiringly towards the truck, they heard the matter-of-fact voice of the policeman announce the death, then they heard Sejosenye say piteously: 'Can't you return those words back?'

She turned away from them, either to collect her wits or the few posses-sions she had brought with her. Her feet and buttocks quivered anxiously as she stumbled towards her hut. Then her feet tripped her up and she fell to the ground like a stunned log.

The people of Ga-Sefete-Molemo ward buried the boy Friedman but none of them would go near the hospital where Sejosenye lay. The stories brought to them by way of the nurses were too terrible for words. They said the old woman sang and laughed and talked to herself all the time. So they merely asked each other: 'Have you been to see Mma-Sejosenye?' 'I'm afraid I cannot. It would kill my heart.' Two weeks later, they buried her.

As was village habit, the incident was discussed thoroughly from all sides till it was understood. In this timeless, sleepy village, the goats stood and suckled their young ones on the main road or lay down and took their afternoon naps there. The motorists either stopped for them or gave way. But it appeared that the driver of the truck had neither brakes on his car nor a driving licence. He belonged to the new, rich civil-servant class whose salaries had become fantastically high since independence. They had to have cars in keeping with their new status; they had to have any car, as long as it was a car; they were in such a hurry about everything that they couldn't be bothered to take driving lessons. And thus progress, development, and a pre-occupation with status and living-standards first announced themselves to the village. It looked like being an ugly story with many decapitated bodies on the main road.

Snapshots of a Wedding

Wedding days always started at the haunting, magical hour of early dawn when there was only a pale crack of light on the horizon. For those who were awake, it took the earth hours to adjust to daylight. The cool and damp of the night slowly arose in shimmering waves like water and even the forms of the people who bestirred themselves at this unearthly hour were distorted in the haze; they appeared to be dancers in slow motion, with fluid, watery forms. In the dim light, four men, the relatives of the bridegroom, Kegoletile, slowly herded an ox before them towards the yard of MmaKhudu, where the bride, Neo, lived. People were already astir in MmaKhudu's yard, yet for a while they all came and peered closely at the distorted fluid forms that approached, to ascertain if it were indeed the relatives of the bridegroom. Then the ox, who was a rather stupid fellow and unaware of his sudden and impending end as meat for the wedding feast, bellowed casually his early morning yawn. At this, the beautiful ululating of the women rose and swelled over the air like water bubbling rapidly and melodiously over the stones of a clear, sparkling stream. In between ululating all the while, the women began to weave about the yard in the wedding dance; now and then they bent over and shook their buttocks in the air. As they handed over the ox, one of the bridegroom's relatives joked:

'This is going to be a modern wedding.' He meant that a lot of the traditional courtesies had been left out of the planning for the wedding day; no one had been awake all night preparing diphiri or the traditional wedding breakfast of pounded meat and samp; the bridegroom said he had no church and did not care about such things; the bride was six months pregnant and showing it, so there was just going to be a quick marriage ceremony at the police camp.

'Oh, we all have our own ways,' one of the bride's relatives joked back.

'If the times are changing, we keep up with them.' And she weaved away ululating joyously.

Whenever there was a wedding the talk and gossip that preceded it were appalling, except that this time the relatives of the bride, Neo, kept their talk a strict secret among themselves. They were anxious to be rid of her; she was an impossible girl with haughty, arrogant ways. Of all her family and relatives, she was the only one who had completed her 'O' levels and she never failed to rub in this fact. She walked around with her nose in the air; illiterate relatives were beneath her greeting—it was done in a clever way, she just turned her head to one side and smiled to herself or when she greeted it was like an insult; she stretched her hand out, palm outspread, swung it down laughing with a gesture that plainly said: 'Oh, that's you!' Only her mother seemed bemused by her education. At her own home Neo was waited on hand and foot. Outside her home nasty remarks were passed. People bitterly disliked conceit and pride.

'That girl has no manners!' the relatives would remark. 'What's the good of education if it goes to someone's head so badly they have no respect for the people? Oh, she is not a person.'

Then they would nod their heads in that fatal way, with predictions that one day life would bring her down. Actually, life had treated Neo rather nicely. Two months after completing her 'O' levels she became pregant by Kegoletile with their first child. It soon became known that another girl, Mathata, was also pregnant by Kegoletile. The difference between the two girls was that Mathata was completely uneducated; the only work she would ever do was that of a housemaid, while Neo had endless opportunities before her—typist, book-keeper, or secretary. So Neo merely smiled; Mathata was no rival. It was as though the decision had been worked out by circumstance because when the families converged on Kegoletile at the birth of the children—he was rich in cattle and they wanted to see what they could get—he of course immediately proposed marriage to Neo; and for Mathata, he agreed to a court order to pay a maintenance of R10.00 a month until the child was twenty years old. Mathata merely smiled too. Girls like her offered no resistance to the approaches of men; when they lost them, they just let things ride.

'He is of course just running after the education and not the manners,' Neo's relatives commented, to show they were not fooled by human nature. 'He thinks that since she is as educated as he is they will both get good jobs and be rich in no time . . .'

Educated as he was, Kegoletile seemed to go through a secret conflict during that year he prepared a yard for his future married life with Neo. He spent most of his free time in the yard of Mathata. His behaviour there wasn't too alarming but he showered Mathata with gifts of all kinds—food, fancy dresses, shoes and underwear. Each time he came, he brought a gift and each time Mathata would burst out laughing and comment: 'Ow, Kego-letile, how can I wear all these dresses? It's just a waste of money! Besides, I manage quite well with the R10.00 you give every month for the child . . .'

She was a very pretty girl with black eyes like stars; she was always smiling and happy; immediately and always her own natural self. He knew what he was marrying—something quite the opposite, a new kind of girl with false postures and acquired, grand-madame ways. And yet, it didn't pay a man these days to look too closely into his heart. They all wanted as wives, women who were big money-earners and they were so ruthless about it! And yet it was as though the society itself stamped each of its individuals with its own particular brand of wealth and Kegoletile had not yet escaped it; he had about him an engaging humility and eagerness to help and please that made him loved and respected by all who knew him. During those times he sat in Mathata's yard, he communicated nothing of the conflict he felt but he would sit on a chair with his arms spread out across its back, turn his head sideways and stare at what seemed to be an empty space beside him. Then he would smile, stand up and walk away. Nothing dramatic. During the year he prepared the huts in his new yard, he frequently slept at the home of Neo.

Relatives on both sides watched this division of interest between the two yards and one day when Neo walked patronizingly into the yard of an aunt, the aunt decided to frighten her a little.

'Well aunt,' she said, with the familiar careless disrespect which went with her so-called, educated, status. 'Will you make me some tea? And how's things?'

The aunt spoke very quietly.

'You may not know it, my girl, but you are hated by everyone around here. The debate we have going is whether a nice young man like Kegoletile should marry bad-mannered rubbish like you. He would be far better off if he married a girl like Mathata, who though uneducated, still treats people with respect.'

The shock the silly girl received made her stare for a terrified moment at her aunt. Then she stood up and ran out of the house. It wiped the superior smile off her face and brought her down a little. She developed an anxiety to greet people and also an anxiety about securing Kegoletile as a husband—

that was why she became pregnant six months before the marriage could take place. In spite of this, her own relatives still disliked her and right up to the day of the wedding they were still debating whether Neo was a suitable wife for any man. No one would have guessed it though with all the dancing, ululating and happiness expressed in the yard and streams of guests gaily ululated themselves along the pathways with wedding gifts precariously balanced on their heads. Neo's maternal aunts, all sedately decked up in shawls, sat in a select group by themselves in a corner of the yard. They sat on the bare ground with their legs stretched out before them but they were served like queens the whole day long. Trays of tea, dry white bread, plates of meat, rice, and salad were constantly placed before them. Their important task was to formally hand over the bride to Kegoletile's maternal aunts when they approached the yard at sunset. So they sat the whole day with still, expressionless faces, waiting to fulfill this ancient rite.

Equally still and expressionless were the faces of the long column of women, Kegoletile's maternal aunts, who appeared outside the yard just as the sun sank low. They walked slowly into the yard indifferent to the ululating that greeted them and seated themselves in a group opposite Neo's maternal aunts. The yard became very silent while each group made its report. Kegoletile had provided all the food for the wedding feast and a maternal aunt from his side first asked:

'Is there any complaint? Has all gone well?'

'We have no complaint,' the opposite party replied.

'We have come to ask for water,' Kegoletile's side said, meaning that from times past the bride was supposed to carry water at her in-law's home.

'It is agreed to,' the opposite party replied.

Neo's maternal aunts then turned to the bridegroom and counselled him: 'Son, you must plough and supply us with corn each year.'

Then Kegoletile's maternal aunts turned to the bride and counselled her: 'Daughter, you must carry water for your husband. Beware, that at all times, he is the owner of the house and must be obeyed. Do not mind if he stops now and then and talks to other ladies. Let him feel free to come and go as he likes . . .'

The formalities over, it was now time for Kegoletile's maternal aunts to get up, ululate and weave and dance about the yard. Then, still dancing and ululating, accompanied by the bride and groom they slowly wound their way to the yard of Kegoletile where another feast had been prepared. As they approached his yard, an old woman suddenly dashed out and chopped at the ground with a hoe. It was all only a formality. Neo would never be the kind of wife who went to the lands to plough. She already had a well-paid job in an office as a secretary. Following on this another old woman took the bride by the hand and led her to a smeared and decorated courtyard wherein had been placed a traditional animal-skin Tswana mat. She was made to sit on the mat and a shawl and kerchief were placed before her. The shawl was ceremonially wrapped around her shoulders; the kerchief tied around her head—the symbols that she was now a married woman.

Guests quietly moved forward to greet the bride. Then two girls started to ululate and dance in front of the bride. As they both turned and bent over to shake their buttocks in the air, they bumped into each other and toppled over. The wedding guests roared with laughter. Neo, who had all this time been stiff, immobile, and rigid, bent forward and her shoulders shook with laughter.

The hoe, the mat, the shawl, the kerchief, the beautiful flute-like ululating of the women seemed in itself a blessing on the marriage but all the guests were deeply moved when out of the crowd, a woman of majestic, regal bearing slowly approached the bride. It was the aunt who had scolded Neo for her bad manners and modern ways. She dropped to her knees before the bride, clenched her fists together and pounded the ground hard with each clenched fist on either side of the bride's legs. As she pounded her fists she said loudly:

'Be a good wife! Be a good wife!'

The Special One

I was a newcomer to the village at that time and teaching at one of the primary schools. Mrs Maleboge was one of my colleagues, a short, stout woman, with a very sad face, who always wore a shawl and a white cotton kerchief wound rather unbecomingly around her head; the kerchief obscured a quarter part of her face so that her sad black eyes stared out from under it. She moved very slowly like the olden-day sailing ships blown by a steady breeze and her speech was as slow and steady as her walk. As soon as one became acquainted with her, she'd start to talk about the great tragedy in her life. Apparently, her husband had left her a small inheritance of cattle at his death, enough to have made her life comfortable in old age. The inheritance had been stolen from her by his brothers and so she was forced to seek employment in her old age when she should have been resting (she was sixty years old). She could stand for about an hour and outline details of the court case she had had with her brothers-in-law, and then stare quietly into the distance and comment: 'I lost it because women are just dogs in this society.' She did it to me twice, pinned me down and made me listen to the story, so that I developed an anxiety to avoid her. It was impossible to say: 'Excuse me, I have to hurry somewhere'—she was too regal and commanded attention once she had started talking.

One day, without any change of expression, she said to me: 'You must come to the baptismal party for my grandchild. It's on Sunday.' Perhaps she didn't mean it, she was just self-absorbed, but her expression implied that the baptismal party was sad too like everything else. She also gave me directions to her home: 'I live near the church. Just get near the church, then ask anyone in the surroundings where I live. They will show you my yard . . .'

So that was what I did, used the church as a guide-mark and then stood looking around, confused. Thousands of little footpaths spread out all round it towards thousands of yards, all with the same look. Where did I go from here? Suddenly along the footpath on which I was standing, a woman came walking towards me. She was walking rather rapidly and in a peculiar way with the wide, swaying footsteps of a drunk. She only cared about herself because she was looking at nothing and she would have walked right past me had I not said, with some desperation: 'Please, do you know the yard of Mrs Maleboge?'

She stopped abruptly in the midst of her wide, swaying walk, turned around and looked directly at me.

'Why do you want to know where Mrs Maleboge lives?' she asked.

'She invited me to the baptismal party of her grandchild,' I replied, uneasily. There was something wrong with the woman and she frightened me a little. To my surprise, she gasped and broke into a very friendly smile.

'How can Mrs Maleboge do this!' she exclaimed. 'I am her best friend and she never told me that she was having a party! I am going to the party too! Come, I'll take you to her home. It's just around the corner.'

That settled me a little and I was enchanted by the way she had had her mind entirely set on going somewhere else, and now had her mind entirely set on going to Mrs Maleboge's party. She had a light chiffon scarf wound around her head and she suddenly wrenched it off and began swinging it to and fro with the rhythm of her walk, like a young girl. I thought she might be in her late thirties and her mat of closely-cropped brown hair clung neatly to her head. She told me later that her name was Gaenametse, which literally translated means there-is-no-water but translated in a figurative way meant that at the time she was born, the marriage between her parents had been very unsatisfactory.

When we entered the yard of Mrs Maleboge, there were quite a number of guests assembled already. The old woman walked straight towards us, looking brighter and brisker than usual and taking me by the arm she said: 'Special guests must enter the hut and be served separately. That is our custom.'

Gaenametse and I entered the hut and as soon as the door was closed, my companion flung herself at Mrs Maleboge and began teasing and joking about the fact that her best friend had not invited her to the party but she was here all the same. They were really old friends, with a dialogue, and as soon as we were seated, Gaenametse picked up the dialogue at the exact point at which it had been left off when they last met.

'He's gone to her again!' she burst out. 'I am at my wit's end, Mma-Maleboge. My love for my husband has reached the over-limit stage. I cannot part from him.'

So acute was her misery that her whole body was shaken by sobs. And I thought: 'That clears up the mystery of her frightening way of walking. She's at the point of breakdown.'

I gathered from what they did next, that they had been through this ritual a number of times. Mrs Maleboge sank to her knees, closed her eyes and began earnestly to implore Jesus to come to the aid of her friend. They formed a touching and complete circle of concentration. Gaenametse did not close her eyes. She stared intently at Mrs Maleboge's face as though expecting her at any moment to make contact with Jesus, and she did not want to miss that moment when it arrived. This effort of concentration so sharpened and heightened every feature in her face that I remember wondering why the unknown husband did not love such a beautiful woman. I had the impression of someone glowing with life, charm, and vitality.

Mrs Maleboge's prayer went on for well over fifteen minutes. Then she stood up and calmly carried on with her duties as hostess of a baptismal party. Neither woman was put out that a stranger had been witness to their private affairs. Gaenametse sat back, relaxed and calm, prepared to enjoy the party. She made some friendly conversation asking who I was and where I had come from. We were both handed plates of rice and chicken and salad by Mrs Maleboge. She had gone up in my estimation. I was deeply moved by the kindness she displayed towards her distressed friend and the touching and almost futile way in which the two women tried to cope with this eternal problem. Towards evening, Mrs Maleboge walked me a little way home and her final comment on the event was:

'Gaenametse has a very bad husband. He is off from woman to woman, but we are praying about the matter,' and she stared quietly and sadly into the distance. She did not have to add that women are just dogs in this society. I believed her by then.

Six months later Gaenametse walked slowly down the road past my home; at least I saw someone I vaguely recognised. She had exchanged the lovely light chiffon scarf for the white cotton kerchief worn by Mrs Maleboge and wound it unbecomingly around her head so that only her eyes peeped out beneath it. A shawl was about her shoulders and her dress reached to the ankles. She had a piece of white crochet work in her hand and worked the crochet needle up and down as she walked. She looked very old and she recognised me more readily than I recognised her. She turned around with that sudden, impulsive movement and friendly smile.

'Oh,' she said. 'So this is where you live,' and she turned in her path and walked straight up to my door.

I made tea, puzzled all the while. I just could not see the wild and beautiful woman of that Sunday. She soon informed me about this chameleon-like change of personality.

'I am divorced from my husband,' she said, with a complacent smile.

'I'm sorry to hear that,' I said, thinking that that was expected of me. I could see that she did not care a damn.

'Oh everything is going to be all right,' she said airily. 'I have need of nothing. My father left me a lot of cattle when he died.'

She put her head to one side, still with that complacent smile, and stroked the dead body of her marriage: 'No one could have loved my husband as much as I did. I loved him too much.'

'It's very sad when such things happen,' I said.

'Oh, life isn't so bad,' she said. 'I can tell you a secret. Even old women like Mrs Maleboge are quite happy. They still make love.'

I was so startled by this that I burst out: 'You don't say!'

She put on the sweet and secret smile of a woman who knows much about this side of life.

'When you are old,' she said, 'that's the time you make love, more than when you are young. You make love because you are no longer afraid of making babies. You make love with young boys. They all do it but it is done very secretly. No one suspects, that is why they look so respectable in the day time.'

It was just a bit beyond my imagination—Mrs Maleboge and a young boy! I shrugged my shoulders, lost. It never occurred to me either that this might also be Gaenametse's preoccupation. After we had drunk tea I walked her a little way down the road, and as I was returning to my own home I was accosted by a woman neighbour.

'What are you doing with *that one*?' she demanded.

I looked back at her, discomforted. It was the height of insult to refer to someone as *that one* but I was a bit appalled by that story of old women and young boys getting together.

'Don't you ever know what's going on in this village?' the gossipy neighbour persisted. 'No one will talk to *her*. She's a wash-out! Everyone knows about her private life. She had a terrible divorce case. She was driving the husband mad. She pestered him day and night for the blankets, and even wanted him to do it during the time she was having her monthly bleeding. Many women have killed men by sleeping with them during that time. It's a dangerous thing and against our custom. The woman will remain alive and the man will die. She was trying to kill the husband, so the court ruled that he'd better be parted from such a terrible woman.'

I stared back at her in petrified horror. She must have thought I understood and approved of some of the insane beliefs of a primitive society, and the society was primitive in certain respects—all primitive societies have their holy fear of a woman's menstrual cycle; during that time she is dirty, and a source of death and danger to the surroundings in general. No, what horrified me was the memory of that Sunday; the wide, drunken swaying walk of extreme emotional distress; the tender appeal two women had made to Jesus for help and a sudden insight into the depth of wickedness of the unknown man. He must have anticipated this social reaction to his wife and deliberately invoked the old tribal taboo to boost his image. How she must have cringed and squirmed, and after the divorce tried to build up an image of respect by dressing up like old Mrs Maleboge! It was impossible to convey all this to the snickering village gossip, so I simply told her quite seriously, without knowing anything definite about it, that where I came from the men usually slept with the women when they were menstruating so it was all right for me to talk to Gaenametse.

Shortly afterwards, I saw Gaenametse in the central shopping area of the village. She was dressed like Mrs Maleboge but she was off her beam again. Her walk was her own, wide, drunken, and swaying. Soon I noticed that she was following a young man and a young girl who were strolling casually down the dusty dirt road, hand in hand. She caught up with the couple and with a swift movement planted herself firmly in their path. She looked at the young man with a terribly ugly expression. Since I could read it, he must have read it too. It said plainly: 'So, I am only good enough to visit at night. I'd like to stroll casually through the village with you, hand in hand.' But no word was exchanged. She turned abruptly and swayed her way off into the distance. She was like that, a wild and wayward learner. She must have decided there and then that Mrs Maleboge's tricks were beyond her. She could not keep her emotions within bounds.

Her last image was the final one I saw. A business matter forced me to take a walk to a remote and far-flung part of the village. While on my way back a voice called out gaily: 'Hey, what are you doing here?' I turned around and there was Gaenametse briskly sweeping a yard with a broom. She was still dressed like Mrs Maleboge but she looked happy in a complacent kind of way, like the day she had walked down the road with her crochet work.

'Won't you come in for some tea?' she asked. 'I watched you walking right to the end of the village and you must be thirsty.'

As we walked towards the single mud hut in the yard, she lowered her voice to a whisper: 'I have a husband. We are not quite married yet, but he is the priest of our church. He started the church himself because he can heal people. I went to him when my heart was troubled and so we found love. He is a very good man. He's inside the house now studying the Bible.'

The man was seated on a low wooden stool. He was quite elderly, with greying hair. He stood up as we entered and politely clasped his hands together, exchanged greetings, and quietly went back to his Bible study. We drank tea, talked, and then she walked with me a little of the way home.

'You seem happy now,' I said. 'I cannot forget how unhappy you were that day at Mrs Maleboge's party.'

She smiled, that sweetly secret smile of a woman who knows how to sort out her love life.

'I have all I need now,' she said. 'I have a good man. I am his mosadi-rra.'

'What does that mean?' I asked.

'It means I am the special one,' she said.

And as I walked on alone I thought that the old days of polygamy are gone and done with, but the men haven't yet accepted that the women want them to be monogamists.

The Collector of Treasures

The long-term central state prison in the south was a whole day's journey away from the villages of the northern part of the country. They had left the village of Puleng at about nine that morning and all day long the police truck droned as it sped southwards on the wide, dusty cross-country track-road. The everyday world of ploughed fields, grazing cattle, and vast expanses of bush and forest seemed indifferent to the hungry eyes of the prisoner who gazed out at them through the wire mesh grating at the back of the police truck. At some point during the journey, the prisoner seemed to strike at some ultimate source of pain and loneliness within her being and, overcome by it, she slowly crumpled forward in a wasted heap, oblivious to everything but her pain. Sunset swept by, then dusk, then dark and still the truck droned on, impersonally, uncaring.

At first, faintly on the horizon, the orange glow of the city lights of the new independence town of Gaborone, appeared like an astonishing phantom in the overwhelming darkness of the bush, until the truck struck tarred roads, neon lights, shops and cinemas, and made the bush a phantom amidst a blaze of light. All this passed untimed, unwatched by the crumpled prisoner; she did not stir as the truck finally droned to a halt outside the prison gates. The torchlight struck the side of her face like an agonising blow. Thinking she was asleep, the policeman called out briskly:

'You must awaken now. We have arrived.'

He struggled with the lock in the dark and pulled open the grating. She crawled painfully forward, in silence.

Together, they walked up a short flight of stairs and waited awhile as the man tapped lightly, several times, on the heavy iron prison door. The night-duty attendant opened the door a crack, peered out and then opened the door a little wider for them to enter. He quietly and casually led the way to a small office, looked at his colleague and asked: 'What do we have here?'

'It's the husband murder case from Puleng village,' the other replied, handing over a file.

The attendant took the file and sat down at a table on which lay open a large record book. In a big, bold scrawl he recorded the details: Dikeledi Mokopi. Charge: Man-slaughter. Sentence: Life. A night-duty wardress appeared and led the prisoner away to a side cubicle, where she was asked to undress.

'Have you any money on you?' the wardress queried, handing her a plain, green cotton dress which was the prison uniform. The prisoner silently shook her head.

'So, you have killed your husband, have you?' the wardress remarked, with a flicker of humour. 'You'll be in good company. We have four other women here for the same crime. It's becoming the fashion these days. Come with me,' and she led the way along a corridor, turned left and stopped at an iron gate which she opened with a key, waited for the prisoner to walk in ahead of her and then locked it with the key again. They entered a small, immensely high-walled courtyard. On one side were toilets, showers, and a cupboard. On the other, an empty concrete quadrangle. The wardress walked to the cupboard, unlocked it and took out a thick roll of clean-smelling blankets which she handed to the prisoner. At the lower end of the walled courtyard was a heavy iron door which led to the cell. The wardress walked up to this door, banged on it loudly and called out: 'I say, will you women in there light your candle?'

A voice within called out: 'All right,' and they could hear the scratch-scratch of a match. The wardress again inserted a key, opened the door and watched for a while as the prisoner spread out her blankets on the floor. The four women prisoners already confined in the cell sat up briefly, and stared silently at their new companion. As the door was locked, they all greeted her quietly and one of the women asked: 'Where do you come from?'

'Puleng', the newcomer replied, and seemingly satisfied with that, the light was blown out and the women lay down to continue their interrupted sleep. And as though she had reached the end of her destination, the new prisoner too fell into a deep sleep as soon as she had pulled her blankets about her.

The breakfast gong sounded at six the next morning. The women stirred themselves for their daily routine. They stood up, shook out their blankets and rolled them up into neat bundles. The day-duty wardress rattled the key in the lock and let them out into the small concrete courtyard so that they could perform their morning toilet. Then, with a loud clatter of pails and plates, two male prisoners appeared at the gate with breakfast. The men handed each woman a plate of porridge and a mug of black tea and they settled themselves on the concrete floor to eat. They turned and looked at their new companion and one of the women, a spokesman for the group said kindly:

'You should take care. The tea has no sugar in it. What we usually do is scoop the sugar off the porridge and put it into the tea.'

The woman, Dikeledi, looked up and smiled. She had experienced such terror during the awaiting-trial period that she looked more like a skeleton than a human being. The skin creaked tautly over her cheeks. The other woman smiled, but after her own fashion. Her face permanently wore a look of cynical, whimsical humour. She had a full, plump figure. She introduced herself and her companions: 'My name is Kebonye. Then that's Otsetswe, Galeboe, and Monwana. What may your name be?'

'Dikeledi Mokopi.'

'How is it that you have such a tragic name,' Kebonye observed. 'Why did your parents have to name you *tears*?'

'My father passed away at that time and it is my mother's tears that I am named after,' Dikeledi said, then added: 'She herself passed away six years later and I was brought up by my uncle.'

Kebonye shook her head sympathetically, slowly raising a spoonful of porridge to her mouth. That swallowed, she asked next:

'And what may your crime be?'

'I have killed my husband.'

'We are all here for the same crime,' Kebonye said, then with her cynical smile asked: 'Do you feel any sorrow about the crime?'

'Not really,' the other woman replied.

'How did you kill him?'

'I cut off all his special parts with a knife,' Dikeledi said.

'I did it with a razor,' Kebonye said. She sighed and added: 'I have had a troubled life.'

A little silence followed while they all busied themselves with their food, then Kebonye continued musingly:

'Our men do not think that we need tenderness and care. You know, my husband used to kick me between the legs when he wanted that. I once aborted with a child, due to this treatment. I could see that there was no way to appeal to him if I felt ill, so I once said to him that if he liked he could keep some other woman as well because I couldn't manage to satisfy all his needs. Well, he was an education-officer and each year he used to suspend about seventeen male teachers for making school girls pregnant, but he used to do the same. The last time it happened the parents of the girl were very angry and came to report the matter to me. I told them: "You leave it to me. I have seen enough." And so I killed him.'

They sat in silence and completed their meal, then they took their plates and cups to rinse them in the wash-room. The wardress produced some pails and a broom. Their sleeping quarters had to be flushed out with water; there was not a speck of dirt anywhere, but that was prison routine. All that was left was an inspection by the director of the prison. Here again Kebonye turned to the newcomer and warned:

'You must be careful when the chief comes to inspect. He is mad about one thing—attention! Stand up straight! Hands at your sides! If this is not done you should see how he stands here and curses. He does not mind anything but that. He is mad about that.'

Inspection over, the women were taken through a number of gates to an open, sunny yard, fenced in by high, barbed-wire where they did their daily work. The prison was a rehabilitation centre where the prisoners produced goods which were sold in the prison store; the women produced garments of cloth and wool; the men did carpentry, shoe-making, brick-making, and vegetable production.

Dikeledi had a number of skills—she could knit, sew, and weave baskets. All the women at present were busy knitting woollen garments; some were learners and did their work slowly and painstakingly. They looked at Dikeledi with interest as she took a ball of wool and a pair of knitting needles and rapidly cast on stitches. She had soft, caressing, almost boneless, hands of strange power—work of a beautiful design grew from those hands. By mid-morning she had completed the front part of a jersey and they all stopped to admire the pattern she had invented in her own head.

'You are a gifted person,' Kebonye remarked, admiringly.

'All my friends say so,' Dikeledi replied smiling. 'You know, I am the woman whose thatch does not leak. Whenever my friends wanted to thatch their huts, I was there. They would never do it without me. I was always busy and employed because it was with these hands that I fed and reared my children. My husband left me after four years of marriage but I managed well enough to feed those mouths. If people did not pay me in money for my work, they paid me with gifts of food.'

'It's not so bad here,' Kebonye said. 'We get a little money saved for us out of the sale of our work, and if you work like that you can still produce money for your children. How many children do you have?'

'I have three sons.'

'Are they in good care?'

'Yes.'

'I like lunch,' Kebonye said, oddly turning the conversation. 'It is the best meal of the day. We get samp and meat and vegetables.'

So the day passed pleasantly enough with chatter and work and at sunset the women were once more taken back to the cell for lock-up time. They unrolled their blankets and prepared their beds, and with the candle lit continued to talk a while longer. Just as they were about to retire for the night, Dikeledi nodded to her new-found friend, Kebonye:

'Thank you for all your kindness to me,' she said, softly.

'We must help each other,' Kebonye replied, with her amused, cynical smile. 'This is a terrible world. There is only misery here.'

And so the woman Dikeledi began phase three of a life that had been ashen in its loneliness and unhappiness. And yet she had always found gold amidst the ash, deep loves that had joined her heart to the hearts of others. She smiled tenderly at Kebonye because she knew already that she had found another such love. She was the collector of such treasures.

* * *

There were really only two kinds of men in the society. The one kind created such misery and chaos that he could be broadly damned as evil. If one watched the village dogs chasing a bitch on heat, they usually moved around in packs of four or five. As the mating progressed one dog would attempt to gain dominance over the festivities and oust all the others from the bitch's vulva. The rest of the hapless dogs would stand around yapping and snapping in its face while the top dog indulged in a continuous spurt of orgasms, day and night until he was exhausted. No doubt, during that Herculean feat, the dog imagined he was the only penis in the world and that there had to be a scramble for it. That kind of man lived near the animal level and behaved just the same. Like the dogs and bulls and donkeys, he also accepted no responsibility for the young he procreated and like the dogs and bulls and donkeys, he also made females abort. Since that kind of man was in the majority in the society, he needed a little analysing as he was responsible for the complete breakdown of family life. He could be analysed over three time-spans. In the old days, before the colonial invasion of Africa, he was a man who lived by the traditions and taboos outlined for all the people by the forefathers of the tribe. He had little individual freedom to assess whether these traditions were compassionate or not—they demanded that he comply and obey the rules, without thought. But when the laws of the ancestors are examined, they appear on the whole to have been vast, external disciplines for the good of the society as a whole, with little attention given to individual preferences and needs. The ancestors made so many errors and one of the most bitter-making things was that they relegated to men a superior position in the tribe, while women were regarded, in a congenital sense, as being an inferior form of human life. To this day, women still suffered from all the calamities that befall an inferior form of human life. The colonial era and the period of migratory mining labour to South Africa was a further affliction visited on this man. It broke the hold of the ancestors. It broke the old, traditional form of family life and for long periods a man was separated from his wife and children while he worked for a pittance in another land in order to raise the money to pay his British Colonial poll-tax. British Colonialism scarcely enriched his life. He then became 'the boy' of the white man and a machine-tool of the South African mines. African independence seemed merely one more affliction on top of the afflictions that had visited this man's life. Independence suddenly and dramatically changed the pattern of colonial subservience. More jobs became available under the new government's localization programme and salaries sky-rocketed at the same time. It provided the first occasion for family life of a new order, above the childlike discipline of custom, the degradation of colonialism. Men and women, in order to survive, had to turn inwards to their own resources. It was the man who arrived at this turning point, a broken wreck with no inner resources at all. It was as though he was hideous to himself and in an effort to flee his own inner emptiness, he spun away from himself in a dizzy kind of death dance of wild destruction and dissipation.

One such man was Garesego Mokopi, the husband of Dikeledi. For four years prior to independence, he had worked as a clerk in the district administration service, at a steady salary of R50.00 a month. Soon after independence his salary shot up to R200.00 per month. Even during his lean days he had had a taste for womanising and drink; now he had the resources for a real spree. He was not seen at home again and lived and slept around the village, from woman to woman. He left his wife and three sons—Banabothe, the eldest, aged four; Inalame, aged three; and the youngest, Motsomi, aged one—to their own resources. Perhaps he did so because she was the boring, semi-literate traditional sort, and there were a lot of exciting new women around. Independence produced marvels indeed.

There was another kind of man in the society with the power to create himself anew. He turned all his resources, both emotional and material, towards his family life and he went on and on with his own quiet rhythm, like a river. He was a poem of tenderness.

One such man was Paul Thebolo and he and his wife, Kenalepe, and their three children, came to live in the village of Puleng in 1966, the year of independence. Paul Thebolo had been offered the principalship of a primary school in the village. They were allocated an empty field beside the yard of Dikeledi Mokopi, for their new home.

Neighbours are the centre of the universe to each other. They help each other at all times and mutually loan each other's goods. Dikeledi Mokopi kept an interested eye on the yard of her new neighbours. At first, only the man appeared with some workmen to erect the fence, which was set up with incredible speed and efficiency. The man impressed her immediately when she went around to introduce herself and find out a little about the new-comers. He was tall, large-boned, slow-moving. He was so peaceful as a person that the sunlight and shadow played all kinds of tricks with his eyes, making it difficult to determine their exact colour. When he stood still and looked reflective, the sunlight liked to creep into his eyes and nestle there; so sometimes his eyes were the colour of shade, and sometimes light brown.

He turned and smiled at her in a friendly way when she introduced herself and explained that he and his wife were on transfer from the village of Bobonong. His wife and children were living with relatives in the village until the yard was prepared. He was in a hurry to settle down as the school term would start in a month's time. They were, he said, going to erect two mud huts first and later he intended setting up a small house of bricks. His wife would be coming around in a few days with some women to erect the mud walls of the huts.

'I would like to offer my help too,' Dikeledi said. 'If work always starts early in the morning and there are about six of us, we can get both walls erected in a week. If you want one of the huts done in woman's thatch, all my friends know that I am the woman whose thatch does not leak.'

The man smilingly replied that he would impart all this information to his wife, then he added charmingly that he thought she would like his wife when they met. His wife was a very friendly person; everyone liked her.

Dikeledi walked back to her own yard with a high heart. She had few callers. None of her relatives called for fear that since her husband had left her she would become dependent on them for many things. The people who called did business with her; they wanted her to make dresses for their children or knit jerseys for the winter time and at times when she had no orders at all, she made baskets which she sold. In these ways she supported herself and the three children but she was lonely for true friends.

All turned out as the husband had said—he had a lovely wife. She was fairly tall and thin with a bright, vivacious manner. She made no effort to conceal that normally, and every day, she was a very happy person. And all turned out as Dikeledi had said. The work-party of six women erected the mud walls of the huts in one week; two weeks later, the thatch was complete. The Thebolo family moved into their new abode and Dikeledi Mokopi moved into one of the most prosperous and happy periods of her life. Her life took a big, wide upward curve. Her relationship with the Thebolo family was more than the usual friendly exchange of neighbours. It was rich and creative.

It was not long before the two women had going one of those deep, affectionate, sharing-everything kind of friendships that only women know how to have. It seemed that Kenalepe wanted endless amounts of dresses made for herself and her three little girls. Since Dikeledi would not accept cash for these services—she protested about the many benefits she received from her good neighbours—Paul Thebolo arranged that she be paid in household goods for these services so that for some years Dikeledi was always assured of her basic household needs—the full bag of corn, sugar, tea, powdered milk, and cooking oil. Kenalepe was also the kind of woman who made the whole world spin around her; her attractive personality attracted a whole range of women to her yard and also a whole range of customers for her dressmaking friend, Dikeledi. Eventually, Dikeledi became swamped with work, was forced to buy a second sewing-machine and employ a helper. The two women did everything together—they were forever together at weddings, funerals, and parties in the village. In their leisure hours they freely discussed all their intimate affairs with each other, so that each knew thoroughly the details of the other's life.

'You are a lucky someone,' Dikeledi remarked one day, wistfully. 'Not everyone has the gift of a husband like Paul.'

'Oh yes,' Kenalepe said happily. 'He is an honest somebody.' She knew a little of Dikeledi's list of woes and queried: 'But why did you marry a man like Garesego? I looked carefully at him when you pointed him out to me near the shops the other day and I could see at one glance that he is a butterfly.'

'I think I mostly wanted to get out of my uncle's yard,' Dikeledi replied. 'I never liked my uncle. Rich as he was, he was a hard man and very selfish.

I was only a servant there and pushed about. I went there when I was six years old when my mother died, and it was not a happy life. All his children despised me because I was their servant. Uncle paid for my education for six years, then he said I must leave school. I longed for more because as you know, education opens up the world for one. Garesego was a friend of my uncle and he was the only man who proposed for me. They discussed it between themselves and then my uncle said: "You'd better marry Garesego because you're just hanging around here like a chain on my neck." I agreed, just to get away from that terrible man. Garesego said at that time that he'd rather be married to my sort than the educated kind because those women were stubborn and wanted to lay down the rules for men. Really, I did not ever protest when he started running about. You know what the other women do. They chase after the man from one hut to another and beat up the girlfriends. The man just runs into another hut, that's all. So you don't really win. I wasn't going to do anything like that. I am satisfied I have children. They are a blessing to me.'

'Oh, it isn't enough,' her friend said, shaking her head in deep sympathy. 'I am amazed at how life imparts its gifts. Some people get too much. Others get nothing at all. I have always been lucky in life. One day my parents will visit—they live in the south—and you'll see the fuss they make over me. Paul is just the same. He takes care of everything so that I never have a day of worry . . .'

The man Paul, attracted as wide a range of male friends as his wife. They had guests every evening; illiterate men who wanted him to fill in tax forms or write letters for them, or his own colleagues who wanted to debate the political issues of the day—there was always something new happening every day now that the country had independence. The two women sat on the edge of these debates and listened with fascinated ears, but they never participated. The following day they would chew over the debates with wise, earnest expressions.

'Men's minds travel widely and boldly,' Kenalepe would comment. 'It makes me shiver the way they freely criticise our new government. Did you hear what Petros said last night? He said he knew all those bastards and they were just a lot of crooks who would pull a lot of dirty tricks. Oh dear! I shivered so much when he said that. The way they talk about the government makes you feel in your bones that this is not a safe world to be in, not like the old days when we didn't have governments. And Lentswe said that ten per cent of the population in England really control all the wealth of the country, while the rest live at starvation level. And he said communism

95

would sort all this out. I gathered from the way they discussed this matter that our government is not in favour of communism. I trembled so much when this became clear to me . . .' She paused and laughed proudly. 'I've heard Paul say this several times: "The British only ruled us for eighty years." I wonder why Paul is so fond of saying that?'

And so a completely new world opened up for Dikeledi. It was so impossibly rich and happy that, as the days went by, she immersed herself more deeply in it and quite overlooked the barrenness of her own life. But it hung there like a nagging ache in the mind of her friend, Kenalepe.

'You ought to find another man,' she urged one day, when they had one of their personal discussions. 'It's not good for a woman to live alone.'

'And who would that be?' Dikeledi asked, disillusioned. 'I'd only be bringing trouble into my life whereas now it is all in order. I have my eldest son at school and I can manage to pay the school fees. That's all I really care about.'

'I mean,' said Kenalepe, 'we are also here to make love and enjoy it.'

'Oh I never really cared for it,' the other replied. 'When you experience the worst of it, it just puts you off altogether.'

'What do you mean by that?' Kenalepe asked, wide-eyed.

'I mean it was just jump on and jump off and I used to wonder what it was all about. I developed a dislike for it.'

'You mean Garesego was like that!' Kenalepe said, flabbergasted. 'Why, that's just like a cock hopping from hen to hen. I wonder what he is doing with all those women. I'm sure they are just after his money and so they flatter him . . .' She paused and then added earnestly: 'That's really all the more reason you should find another man. Oh, if you knew what it was really like, you would long for it, I can tell you! I sometimes think I enjoy that side of life far too much. Paul knows a lot about all that. And he always has some new trick with which to surprise me. He has a certain way of smiling when he has thought up something new and I shiver a little and say to myself: "Ha, what is Paul going to do tonight!" '

Kenalepe paused and smiled at her friend, slyly.

'I can loan Paul to you if you like,' she said, then raised one hand to block the protest on her friend's face. 'I would do it because I have never had a friend like you in my life before whom I trust so much. Paul had other girls you know, before he married me, so it's not such an uncommon thing to him. Besides, we used to make love long before we got married and I never got pregnant. He takes care of that side too. I wouldn't mind loaning him because I am expecting another child and I don't feel so well these days . . .'

Dikeledi stared at the ground for a long moment, then she looked up at her friend with tears in her eyes.

'I cannot accept such a gift from you,' she said, deeply moved. 'But if you are ill I will wash for you and cook for you.'

Not put off by her friend's refusal of her generous offer, Kenalepe mentioned the discussion to her husband that very night. He was so taken off-guard by the unexpectedness of the subject that at first he looked slightly astonished, and burst out into loud laughter and for such a lengthy time that he seemed unable to stop.

'Why are you laughing like that?' Kenalepe asked, surprised.

He laughed a bit more, then suddenly turned very serious and thoughtful and was lost in his own thoughts for some time. When she asked him what he was thinking he merely replied: 'I don't want to tell you everything. I want to keep some of my secrets to myself.'

The next day Kenalepe reported this to her friend.

'Now whatever does he mean by that? I want to keep some of my secrets to myself?'

'I think,' Dikeledi said smiling, 'I think he has a conceit about being a good man. Also, when someone loves someone too much, it hurts them to say so. They'd rather keep silent.'

Shortly after this Kenalepe had a miscarriage and had to be admitted to hospital for a minor operation. Dikeledi kept her promise 'to wash and cook' for her friend. She ran both their homes, fed the children and kept everything in order. Also, people complained about the poorness of the hospital diet and each day she scoured the village for eggs and chicken, cooked them, and took them to Kenalepe every day at the lunch-hour.

One evening Dikeledi ran into a snag with her routine. She had just dished up supper for the Thebolo children when a customer came around with an urgent request for an alteration on a wedding dress. The wedding was to take place the next day. She left the children seated around the fire eating and returned to her own home. An hour later, her own children asleep and settled, she thought she would check the Thebolo yard to see if all was well there. She entered the children's hut and noted that they had put themselves to bed and were fast asleep. Their supper plates lay scattered and unwashed around the fire. The hut which Paul and Kenalepe shared was in darkness. It meant that Paul had not yet returned from his usual evening visit to his wife. Dikeledi collected the plates and washed them, then poured the dirty dishwater on the still-glowing embers of the outdoor fire. She piled the plates one on top of the other and carried them to the third additional hut which was used as a kitchen. Just then Paul Thebolo entered the yard, noted the lamp and movement in the kitchen hut and walked over to it. He paused at the open door.

'What are you doing now, Mma-Banabothe?' he asked, addressing her affectionately in the customary way by the name of her eldest son, Banabothe.

'I know quite well what I am doing,' Dikeledi replied happily. She turned around to say that it was not a good thing to leave dirty dishes standing overnight but her mouth flew open with surprise. Two soft pools of cool liquid light were in his eyes and something infinitely sweet passed between them; it was too beautiful to be love.

'You are a very good woman, Mma-Banabothe,' he said softly.

It was the truth and the gift was offered like a nugget of gold. Only men like Paul Thebolo could offer such gifts. She took it and stored another treasure in her heart. She bowed her knee in the traditional curtsey and walked quietly away to her own home.

★ ★ ★

Eight years passed for Dikeledi in a quiet rhythm of work and friendship with the Thebolo's. The crisis came with the eldest son, Banabothe. He had to take his primary school leaving examination at the end of the year. This serious event sobered him up considerably as like all boys he was very fond of playtime. He brought his books home and told his mother that he would like to study in the evenings. He would like to pass with a 'Grade A' to please her. With a flushed and proud face Dikeledi mentioned this to her friend, Kenalepe.

'Banabothe is studying every night now,' she said. 'He never really cared for studies. I am so pleased about this that I bought him a spare lamp and removed him from the children's hut to my own hut where things will be peaceful for him. We both sit up late at night now. I sew on buttons and fix hems and he does his studies . . .'

She also opened a savings account at the post office in order to have some standby money to pay the fees for his secondary education. They were rather high—R85.00. But in spite of all her hoarding of odd cents, towards the end of the year, she was short on R20.00 to cover the fees. Midway during the Christmas school holidays the results were announced. Banabothe passed with a 'Grade A'. His mother was almost hysterical in her joy at his achievement. But what to do? The two youngest sons had already started primary school and she would never manage to cover all their fees from her resources.

She decided to remind Garesego Mokopi that he was the father of the children. She had not seen him in eight years except as a passer-by in the village. Sometimes he waved but he had never talked to her or enquired about her life or that of the children. It did not matter. She was a lower form of human life. Then this unpleasant something turned up at his office one day, just as he was about to leave for lunch. She had heard from village gossip, that he had eventually settled down with a married woman who had a brood of children of her own. He had ousted her husband, in a typical village sensation of brawls, curses, and abuse. Most probably the husband did not care because there were always arms outstretched towards a man, as long as he looked like a man. The attraction of this particular woman for Garesego Mokopi, so her former lovers said with a snicker, was that she went in for heady forms of love-making like biting and scratching.

Garesego Mokopi walked out of his office and looked irritably at the ghost from his past, his wife. She obviously wanted to talk to him and he walked towards her, looking at his watch all the while. Like all the new 'success men', he had developed a paunch, his eyes were blood-shot, his face was bloated, and the odour of the beer and sex from the previous night clung faintly around him. He indicated with his eyes that they should move around to the back of the office block where they could talk in privacy.

'You must hurry with whatever you want to say,' he said impatiently. 'The lunch-hour is very short and I have to be back at the office by two.'

Not to him could she talk of the pride she felt in Banabothe's achievement, so she said simply and quietly: 'Garesego, I beg you to help me pay Banabothe's fees for secondary school. He has passed with a "Grade A" and as you know, the school fees must be produced on the first day of school or else he will be turned away. I have struggled to save money the whole year but I am short by R20.00.'

She handed him her post office savings book, which he took, glanced at and handed back to her. Then he smiled, a smirky know-all smile, and thought he was delivering her a blow in the face.

'Why don't you ask Paul Thebolo for the money?' he said. 'Everyone knows he's keeping two homes and that you are his spare. Everyone knows about that full bag of corn he delivers to your home every six months so why can't he pay the school fees as well?'

She neither denied this, nor confirmed it. The blow glanced off her face which she raised slightly, in pride. Then she walked away.

As was their habit, the two women got together that afternoon and Dikeledi reported this conversation with her husband to Kenalepe who

99

tossed back her head in anger and said fiercely: 'The filthy pig himself! He thinks every man is like him, does he? I shall report this matter to Paul, then he'll see something.'

And indeed Garesego did see something but it was just up his alley. He was a female prostitute in his innermost being and like all professional prostitutes, he enjoyed publicity and sensation—it promoted his cause. He smiled genially and expansively when a madly angry Paul Thebolo came up to the door of his house where he lived with *his* concubine. Garesego had been through a lot of these dramas over those eight years and he almost knew by rote the dialogue that would follow.

'You bastard!' Paul Thebolo spat out. 'Your wife isn't my concubine, do you hear?'

'Then why are you keeping her in food?' Garesego drawled. 'Men only do that for women they fuck! They never do it for nothing.'

Paul Thebolo rested one hand against the wall, half dizzy with anger, and he said tensely: 'You defile life, Garesego Mokopi. There's nothing else in your world but defilement. Mma-Banabothe makes clothes for my wife and children and she will never accept money from me so how else must I pay her?'

'It only proves the story both ways,' the other replied, vilely. 'Women do that for men who fuck them.'

Paul Thebolo shot out the other hand, punched him soundly in one grinning eye and walked away. Who could hide a livid, swollen eye? To every surprised enquiry, he replied with an injured air:

'It was done by my wife's lover, Paul Thebolo.'

It certainly brought the attention of the whole village upon him, which was all he really wanted. Those kinds of men were the bottom rung of government. They secretly hungered to be the President with all eyes on them. He worked up the sensation a little further. He announced that he would pay the school fees of the child of his concubine, who was also to enter secondary school, but not the school fees of his own child, Banabothe. People half liked the smear on Paul Thebolo; he was too good to be true. They delighted in making him a part of the general dirt of the village, so they turned on Garesego and scolded: 'Your wife might be getting things from Paul Thebolo but it's beyond the purse of any man to pay the school fees of his own children as well as the school fees of another man's children. Banabothe wouldn't be there had you not procreated him, Garesego, so it is your duty to care for him. Besides, it's your fault if your wife takes another man. You left her alone all these years.'

So that story was lived with for two weeks, mostly because people wanted to say that Paul Thebolo was a part of life too and as uncertain of his morals as they were. But the story took such a dramatic turn that it made all the men shudder with horror. It was some weeks before they could find the courage to go to bed with women; they preferred to do something else.

Garesego's obscene thought processes were his own undoing. He really believed that another man had a stake in his hen-pen and like any cock, his hair was up about it. He thought he'd walk in and re-establish his own claim to it and so, after two weeks, once the swelling in his eye had died down, he espied Banabothe in the village and asked him to take a note to his mother. He said the child should bring a reply. The note read: 'Dear Mother, I am coming home again so that we may settle our differences. Will you prepare a meal for me and some hot water that I might take a bath. Gare.'

Dikeledi took the note, read it and shook with rage. All its overtones were clear to her. He was coming home for some sex. They had had no differences. They had not even talked to each other.

'Banabothe,' she said. 'Will you play nearby? I want to think a bit then I will send you to your father with the reply.'

Her thought processes were not very clear to her. There was something she could not immediately touch upon. Her life had become holy to her during all those years she had struggled to maintain herself and the children. She had filled her life with treasures of kindness and love she had gathered from others and it was all this that she wanted to protect from defilement by an evil man. Her first panic-stricken thought was to gather up the children and flee the village. But where to go? Garesego did not want a divorce, she had left him to approach her about the matter, she had desisted from taking any other man. She turned her thoughts this way and that and could find no way out except to face him. If she wrote back, don't you dare put foot in the yard I don't want to see you, he would ignore it. Black women didn't have that kind of power. A thoughtful, brooding look came over her face. At last, at peace with herself, she went into her hut and wrote a reply: 'Sir, I shall prepare everything as you have said. Dikeledi.'

It was about midday when Banabothe sped back with the reply to his father. All afternoon Dikeledi busied herself making preparations for the appearance of her husband at sunset. At one point Kenalepe approached the yard and looked around in amazement at the massive preparations, the large iron water pot full of water with a fire burning under it, the extra cooking pots on the fire. Only later Kenalepe brought the knife into focus. But it was only a vague blur, a large kitchen knife used to cut meat and Dikeledi knelt at a grinding-stone and sharpened it slowly and methodically. What was in focus then was the final and tragic expression on the upturned face of her friend. It threw her into confusion and blocked their usual free and easy feminine chatter. When Dikeledi said: 'I am making some preparations for Garesego. He is coming home tonight,' Kenalepe beat a hasty retreat to her own home terrified. They knew they were involved because when she mentioned this to Paul he was distracted and uneasy for the rest of the day. He kept on doing upside-down sorts of things, not replying to questions, absent-mindedly leaving a cup of tea until it got quite cold, and every now and again he stood up and paced about, lost in his own thoughts. So deep was their sense of disturbance that towards evening they no longer made a pretence of talking. They just sat in silence in their hut. Then, at about nine o'clock, they heard those wild and agonized bellows. They both rushed out together to the yard of Dikeledi Mokopi.

*   *   *

He came home at sunset and found everything ready for him as he had requested, and he settled himself down to enjoy a man's life. He had brought a pack of beer along and sat outdoors slowly savouring it while every now and then his eye swept over the Thebolo yard. Only the woman and children moved about the yard. The man was out of sight. Garesego smiled to himself, pleased that he could crow as loud as he liked with no answering challenge.

A basin of warm water was placed before him to wash his hands and then Dikeledi served him his meal. At a separate distance she also served the children and then instructed them to wash and prepare for bed. She noted that Garesego displayed no interest in the children whatsoever. He was entirely wrapped up in himself and thought only of himself and his own comfort. Any tenderness he offered the children might have broken her and swerved her mind away from the deed she had carefully planned all that afternoon. She was beneath his regard and notice too for when she eventually brought her own plate of food and sat near him, he never once glanced at her face. He drank his beer and cast his glance every now and again at the Thebolo yard. Not once did the man of the yard appear until it became too dark to distinguish anything any more. He was completely satisfied with that. He could repeat the performance every day until he broke the mettle of the other cock again and forced him into angry abuse. He liked that sort of thing.

'Garesego, do you think you could help me with Banabothe's school fees?'

Dikeledi asked at one point.

'Oh, I'll think about it,' he replied casually.

She stood up and carried buckets of water into the hut, which she poured into a large tin bath that he might bathe himself, then while he took his bath she busied herself tidying up and completing the last of the household chores. Those done, she entered the children's hut. They played hard during the day and they had already fallen asleep with exhaustion. She knelt down near their sleeping mats and stared at them for a long while, with an extremely tender expression. Then she blew out their lamp and walked to her own hut. Garesego lay sprawled across the bed in such a manner that indicated he only thought of himself and did not intend sharing the bed with anyone else. Satiated with food and drink, he had fallen into a deep, heavy sleep the moment his head touched the pillow. His concubine had no doubt taught him that the correct way for a man to go to bed, was naked. So he lay, unguarded and defenceless, sprawled across the bed on his back.

The bath made a loud clatter as Dikeledi removed it from the room, but still he slept on, lost to the world. She re-entered the hut and closed the door. Then she bent down and reached for the knife under the bed which she had merely concealed with a cloth. With the precision and skill of her hard-working hands, she grasped hold of his genitals and cut them off with one stroke. In doing so, she slit the main artery which ran on the inside of the groin. A massive spurt of blood arched its way across the bed. And Garesego bellowed. He bellowed his anguish. Then all was silent. She stood and watched his death anguish with an intent and brooding look, missing not one detail of it. A knock on the door stirred her out of her reverie. It was the boy, Banabothe. She opened the door and stared at him, speechless. He was trembling violently.

'Mother,' he said, in a terrified whisper. 'Didn't I hear father cry?'

'I have killed him,' she said, waving her hand in the air with a gesture that said—well, that's that. Then she added sharply: 'Banabothe, go and call the police.'

He turned and fled into the night. A second pair of footsteps followed hard on his heels. It was Kenalepe running back to her own yard, half out of her mind with fear. Out of the dark Paul Thebolo stepped towards the hut and entered it. He took in every detail and then he turned and looked at Dikeledi with such a tortured expression that for a time words failed him. At last he said: 'You don't have to worry about the children, Mma-Banabothe. I'll take them as my own and give them all a secondary school education.'

Hunting

The month of July is the hunting season. It is favoured for a number of reasons. The June harvest would be over by then; everyone had corn by that time and they were all looking for something tasty to eat the corn with. It was usually at this time too that all the animals, especially in a year of good rain, were very fat. July was also the coolest month of the whole year and it meant that when the men strung up the meat to dry, it would not rot or get riddled with worms, as it often did in summer. So, suddenly in July, there would be a great exodus of all the men from the everyday round of their village life; sometimes for one week, sometimes for one month. In deep bush, they lived a rough life. They built mosasana or rough bush houses; they cut branches, arranged them in a triangular shape, covered them with grass and crawled into them at night for rest and shelter from the cold. If they were hunting in lion country, they lit big fires at night to frighten the lions away from their rough camps. They all had their own rifles. They killed springbok and hartebeest and brought home enough meat to feed their families for three to four months. Hunting parties were usually composed of groups of four to five men. They kept the groups small like that, they said, because it was not good for the animals to smell the people. They would run away.

Four men, Rapula, Tebogo, Lesedi, and Kelebone, kept an anxious watch on the yard of the man, Tholo. Tholo was the only man in their village ward who owned a tractor with a trailer, and because of this, every man wanted to go hunting with Tholo. When they went out on Tholo's tractor, it meant only one or two days of roughing it in the bush, then they returned with the wet meat and dried it at their leisure in their own yards. They lost nothing of their kill because their wives started by cooking the bones to which bits of meat clung.

At last, two of the men, Rapula and Tebogo, could contain their impatience no longer. They walked into the yard of Tholo. He was busy cleaning and repairing his tractor which had just returned from the lands with the June harvest of corn.

'When will we be leaving, Tholo?' Rapula asked.

The man, Tholo, looked up quietly from his work. He smiled at them, but only with his eyes. He was very tall and thin.

'Are you coming with me this time?' he asked, in a casual and friendly way.

'Yes,' Rapula replied. 'And Lesedi and Kelebone are coming as well.'

Tholo nodded with perfect comprehension. The men drew lots as to whom should go hunting with him each season, so that the good fortune of hunting wild animals with a tractor could be experienced by every man in the village.

'Let us get up early tomorrow morning and leave for the bush,' Tholo said. Then he turned back to his work. That was his way—no gossip or idle chatter.

The two men turned to leave. When they were safely beyond hearing distance, Rapula, who was short, thick-set and chunky, with a sense of humour, burst out into a chuckle:

'I can't understand Tholo,' he said. 'I don't know whether he is a girl or what. Where did you ever see such grand ways?' And he mimicked Tholo's air of lofty surprise and friendliness: '"Are you coming with me this time . . .?" He is just like a chief but here he is living like everyone else.'

'Kelebone might have spoken the truth about a man like Tholo,' Tebogo said thoughtfully. 'He was saying the other day that a man like that has the true power of life in him. We are lucky to have such a good man living with us . . .'

That was what every man knew about Tholo—that he was a good man. He never refused a request for help and shared generously all he had with others. But beyond that the man in him seemed to run away from all the conflicts of life. There was no order or goodness in human life, but there was an order and soundness in everything he could control or communicate with. He communicated deeply, with his wife, and his work.

He had chosen his wife, Thato, carefully. On the surface she looked ordinary, quiet, and withdrawn. But all the women knew that both husband and wife were alike in their generosity. Thato would part with anything she had, on request. When Tholo had begun courting her, she already had a child, a girl, by a man who had deserted her. It was such a common experience for most women these days. Most men insisted that some sort of sexual relationship led to marriage. This trick seemed to be the only way they could get their sex for free. They were not particularly interested in the women and they certainly did not value them. They never gave a thought to the damage they were inflicting on the women—women became hard and callous with no values or tenderness or respect to cling to. Thato had summarized the experience for Tholo, early on in their relationship. She did not resent having the child—no one resented children, but she did resent the trickery and untruthfulness of the men.

'Uneducated women,' she had said, in an exact, precise way. 'They are just there to be misused by men. The men all want to marry educated women, and still they treat them badly. Those women work for them and support them and get no happiness out of marriage . . .'

She had paused, and added a little uncertainly: 'I had waited a long time for marriage. Then I decided to have the child because I might have grown old without having any children . . .'

She had turned at that point to attend to the fire and stirred the pot of porridge cooking over it with the air of one who had dismissed the whole matter from her mind. That was how she tended to treat their relationship in the beginning—matter-of-factly and something she ought to dismiss from her mind. It cost a woman too much to love a man.

They had first met when her mother had engaged Tholo to plough up their land with his tractor. It was the first time a tractor had ever turned up their land. Formerly, and for many years, they had engaged a man with oxen and a single-furrow hand plough to turn up their land. (Their yard was a yard of women only; Thato's father had died when she was still quite young and she lived with her mother and two younger sisters.) It had been such a new and intoxicating experience watching the tractor turn up the land; the perfume of the newly-wet earth arose and floated everywhere and the man's work was compact and professional, just the way he had been taught in the agricultural demonstration school he attended. By late afternoon he had ploughed up all their land and left with his tractor for some other engagement. By night, an unmoving image had haunted her dreams of a man's head turned sideways in fixed concentration as he closely watched the contours and furrows he created behind him. She had cried a little to herself; he had seemed a creature too far removed from her own humble life. There were so many women like her who could work and plough and life wasn't going to offer them any spectacular rewards.

They couldn't say they were strangers and she met him again, after the ploughing season in a store in the village. Love is such a foolhardy feeling. A woman might say: 'They are all the same. He'll come around for two months and then go away forever. But I did not care about the other man and he has some other woman now. It cannot hurt me . . .' So she agreed to a love relationship with the man, Tholo, on that basis, not seeing anything of certainty for the future. Something began to go wrong after two months—he was a man who aroused worship, not love. A deep depression fell upon her and one evening when he came around, she was so withdrawn and moody that she barely greeted him.

'What's wrong?' he had asked, in his quiet way.

She had stared for a few moments with an intense concentration at the fire near which they were seated, and suddenly came to a snap decision. It was a question of letting go of him, so she thought to herself: 'Agh, I'll tell him I'm expecting a child. I hate them all anyway.' So she said it defiantly and angrily and he kept very silent. She had picked up a piece of firewood and begun to draw sharp, nervous straight lines in the ground. When he spoke, his words seemed to reach or walk straight into her tortured mind.

'We can get married,' he said softly. 'I can arrange everything.'

She had shaken her head a little against the unexpected impact of his beautiful life which had quite quickly come so close to her own life. Then she had laughed a bit, relieved, peaceful. Marriage today was not usually arranged by the parents, as in times past. Men and women now made their own agreements to take each other as husband and wife.

'I have nothing to offer you Tholo,' she had said humbly. 'As you can see we are very poor here. I can only plough.'

She had turned and stared at his face in wonder. He was only smiling, with his eyes. It was to take her some time to sort out that smile; it meant that he was incapable of hurting life, that basically he cared about everything. Much later they were going to get their kind of communication going; about crops, about cattle, about people. But that evening he had hesitated to say all he had to say. They were living with that uncertain story of independence. It offered advantages to all men which had not been there a few years ago. Farmers and cattlemen like he, were important. He had joined a government agricultural training scheme and been allocated a special demonstrator to work side by side with him, on his lands and at his cattle-post. It often mattered if a man could grasp each opportunity or new idea that was presented to him. She was the kind of woman who could share that life with him.

When he had presented her to his family, they had disliked her for the very reasons he needed her as his wife. One of his aunts had summed it up: 'She is a woman who has seen life. And she's far too old . . .'

They meant, that by the expression of wisdom on Thato's face, she was a woman who could think. Apparently, when a man married, he had to marry a gay and frivolous plaything with an empty head and ten years his junior. Then they wondered about all the futile marriages that barely lasted six months or a year!

They had been married for three years and the whole rhythm and happiness of their lives was tied up in work and their involvements in the needs of other people. Not long after the two men, Rapula and Tebogo, had left the yard, Thato entered with a water-bucket on her head. Tholo looked up again from his work and she, sensing some request, turned and walked towards him. She swung the water bucket down to the ground, near the tractor.

'Will you prepare some provisions?' he said. 'I'm going hunting tomorrow with Rapula, Tebogo, Lesedi, and Kelebone.'

She rested one hand softly on the tractor: 'The animals will be very fat this year,' she said. 'Even our pumpkins and water-melons look sick. They are of an abnormal size.'

Early the next morning, as they had planned, the five men set off on their hunting trip. As always, after a season of good rain, only soft winds blew over the land. By July, one still, blue day followed another and the whole earth seemed temporarily to turn in on itself and fall asleep in the vague warmth of the winter sun. The honey-coloured dry grass danced in the soft breeze like thousands of little girls swishing their tiny skirts. It was in this leisurely atmosphere that the five men hunted. By mid-morning of the second day they had killed all the animals they needed and they returned home by late afternoon. There was a bustle until well past sundown in all their yards. The children all feasted on meat roasted over the coals until their stomachs nearly burst, and long after they had retired the adults sat around the outdoor fires where the bones were still cooking in great iron pots; they had guests coming in the next morning to sample a bit of the kill.

Tholo always loved this part of the day in his own yard. The same scene had been repeated so many times. He sat on a low chair, his wife sat flat on the ground, one leg folded under her, one leg stretched out and she always stared reflectively at the fire.

'What's the news?' he'd say at some point.

She had the capacity to live with the conflicts of life in a way he had not. Like all women, she was involved in village gossip and disputes. She knew everything, but the richness of her communication lay in her gift to sift and sort out all the calamities of everyday life with the unerring heart of a good story-teller. And as though that were the crux of it all, he liked to comment at some point: 'People don't know how to treat each other nicely.'

In response to his question that evening, 'What's the news?' she began: 'Word came today from the cattle-post that one of the young bulls that has not yet been castrated, was involved in a fight with one of the older bulls and has been badly injured . . .' She paused a bit and furrowed her brow. There was some trouble in their village ward. 'There's trouble again between Felicia and her husband. It's a pity because they are just newly married, but Felicia was never very normal, even before marriage. She used to be polite then, but since her marriage she took to quarrelling with her husband every day. People hear nothing but shouting from their yard. She refused to plough this year because she said her husband had a good job and she didn't see why she couldn't rest a bit. Now it appears that the husband isn't very normal either. Today, he resigned from that good job and said he would rest a bit too, since resting and idling was all that was going on in his yard. No one knows how this mess is going to be sorted out but the day they are starving, people will have to help . . .'

And so her voice murmured on relating the incredible muddle and non-sense people made of their lives each day. From her he knew also that not so long ago Rapula had taken up with a shebeen queen and arrived home dead drunk every other night and beat his wife because she complained and scolded. What could be done? Nothing could sort out the world. It would always be a painful muddle. That was why he had turned to Rapula and smiled like God, in a kind and friendly way.

THE AFRICAN AND CARIBBEAN WRITERS SERIES

The book you have been reading is part of Heinemann's long-established series of African and Caribbean fiction. Details of some of the other titles available are given below, but for a catalogue giving information on the whole series write to: Heinemann International Literature and Textbooks, Halley Court, Jordan Hill, Oxford OX2 8EJ

BESSIE HEAD
When Rain Clouds Gather

When a political refugee from South Africa joins forces with an English agricultural expert, the old farming methods and way of life in a poverty-stricken Botswanan village are challenged. The pressures of tradition, the opposition of the local chief and, above all, the harsh climate, threaten to bring tragedy to the community.

Maru

Margaret Cadmore, an orphaned Masarwa girl, comes to Dilepe to teach, only to discover that in this remote Botswanan village her own people are treated as outcasts. Her presence divides the village. In the love story and intrigue that follows, Bessie Head brilliantly combines a portrait of loneliness with a rich affirmation of the mystery and spirituality of life. Her concern for the lot of ordinary people has the sharp authenticity of personal experience.

A Question of Power

'She brilliantly develops ascending degrees of personal isolation, and is very moving when she describes abating pain. Her novels – and this is the third – have a way of soaring up from rock bottom to the stars, and are very shaking.' *Sunday Times*

CHINUA ACHEBE
Anthills of the Savannah

'In a powerful fusion of myth, legend and modern styles Achebe
has written a book which is wise, exciting and essential,
a powerful antidote to the cynical commentators from
"overseas" who see nothing ever new out of Africa.'
The Financial Times

Arrow of God

An account of how a chief priest finds his authority under threat
from many sides, but, believing he is merely an arrow in the
bow of his God, is prepared to lead his people on.

Things Fall Apart

This, the first title in the African Writers Series, describes how a
man in the Igbo tribe of South Africa became exiled from the
tribe and returned to face the tragic consequences of his rash
courage against the white man.

No Longer At Ease

In this intriguing novel, Achebe uses the 'fall' of one man,
a descendant of the hero in *Things Fall Apart*, to depict the birth
of a whole new age in Nigerian life; a powerful, disillusioning
age of corruption.

NGŨGĨ WA THIONG'O
Matigari

This is a moral fable telling the story of a freedom fighter and
his quest for Truth and Justice. Set in the political dawn of post-
independence Kenya.
'Clear, subtle, mischievous passionate novel'. *Sunday Times*

Devil on the Cross

Written secretly in prison, on lavatory paper, while the author
was detained without trial, the novel is a powerful critique of
modern Kenya.

A Grain of Wheat

'With Mr Ngũgĩ, history is living tissue. He writes with poise from deep reserves, and the book adds cubits to his already considerable stature.' *The Guardian*

Petals of Blood

A compelling novel about the tragedy of corrupting power, set in post-independence Kenya.
'. . . Ngũgĩ writes with passion about every form, shape and colour which power can take'. *Sunday Times*

Weep Not, Child

This powerful, moving story about the effects of the Mau Mau war on the lives of ordinary men and women in Kenya is one of the best-known of Ngũgĩ's works.
'This story is a skilful work of art.' *TLS*

The River Between

'A sensitive novel about the Gikuyu in the melting pot that sometimes touches the grandeur of tap-root simplicity.'
The Guardian

STEVE BIKO
I Write What I Like

'An impressive tribute to the depth and range of his thought, covering such diverse issues as the basic philosophy of black consciousness, Bantustans, African culture, the institutional church, and Western involvement in apartheid.'
The Catholic Herald

NELSON MANDELA
No Easy Walk to Freedom

A collection of the articles, speeches, letters and trials of the most important figure in the South African liberation struggle.

OLIVER TAMBO
Preparing for Power – Oliver Tambo Speaks

This selection of speeches, interviews and letters offers a unique insight into the ANC Chairman's views on the history of the freedom struggle within South Africa and, of even greater importance, his vision for the future.

DORIS LESSING
The Grass is Singing

The classic murder story of the Rhodesian farmer's wife and her houseboy.

NADINE GORDIMER
Some Monday for Sure

Nadine Gordimer has used these stories from her five collections to tell of the daily frustrations and contradictions of life in South African society.

AMECHI AKWANYA
Orimili

Set in a complex Nigerian community that's at the point of irrevocable change, this is the story of a man's struggle to be accepted in the company of his town's elders.

SHIMMER CHINODYA
Harvest of Thorns

'Zimbabwe has fine black writers and Shimmer Chinodya is one of the best. *Harvest of Thorns* brilliantly pictures the transition between the old white dominated Southern Rhodesia, through the Bush War, to the new black regime. It is a brave book, a good strong story, and it is often very funny. People who know the country will salute its honesty, but I hope newcomers to African writing will give this book a try. They won't be disappointed.'
Doris Lessing